The Garden Bird Book

The British Trust for Ornithology, in collaboration with whom *The Garden Bird Book* has been produced, was founded in 1933 to help and encourage amateur ornithologists to get more satisfaction out of their birdwatching by undertaking simple research. By asking large numbers of birdwatchers to contribute a few items of information from their own observations, a complete picture can be built up. In this way research by amateurs, as in the BTO's Garden Bird Feeding Survey, which has provided much of the material for this book, can be of immeasurable interest and value to both professional ornithologists and ordinary bird lovers.

David E. Glue, the editor of this book, trained as a zoologist at London University and joined the BTO as a Research Officer in the Population and Surveys Section in 1968. Confined to a wheelchair following a car crash in 1971, he developed a special interest in garden birds. His other research interests are the biology of owls and the bird communities of man-made habitats.

The Garden Bird Book

Edited by David Glue

MACMILLAN LONDON

in association with the
British Trust for Ornithology

First published in hardback 1982 by
Macmillan London Limited

First published in paperback 1984 by
PAPERMAC
a division of Macmillan Publishers Limited
4 Little Essex Street London WC2R 3LF
and Basingstoke

Associated companies in Auckland, Dallas, Delhi, Dublin,
Hong Kong, Johannesburg, Lagos, Manzini, Melbourne,
Nairobi, New York, Singapore, Tokyo, Washington and
Zaria

Composition in Apollo by Filmtype Services Limited,
Scarborough, North Yorkshire

Printed in Hong Kong

ISBN 0 333 36765 0

Contents

The Contributors

PETER G. DAVIS is a professional horticulturalist living near Haslemere in Surrey. His ornithological work has included organising the BTO's national Nightingale Survey in 1980 and writing a technical manual for ringers. His fieldwork has centred around studies of heathland birds and especially the breeding biology of the Stonechat.

DAVID E. GLUE trained as a zoologist at London University and joined the BTO as a Research Officer in the Populations and Surveys Section in 1968. Confined to a wheelchair following a car crash in 1971, he developed a special interest in garden birds. His other research interests include the biology of owls and the bird communities of man-made habitats.

GEOFFREY H. GUSH is an experienced Devon conservation naturalist who has ringed birds and studied their feeding habits for over twenty years. He has supported the Garden Bird Feeding Survey (see p. 5) since its inception and has attracted some eighty-five species to take food or water in his splendid garden.

H.G. HURRELL MBE (1902–81) was a West Country naturalist of great distinction. Author of books on otters and pine martens and a contributor to early BBC *Look* programmes, he instigated the Devon Birdwatching and Preservation Society's survey of birds' drinking and bathing behaviour. His many scientific papers include the report of the BTO's Swift Migration investigation.

CHRISTOPHER J. MEAD, a Senior Research Officer at the BTO, is an expert on garden and woodland titmice populations. His voice is well known to many since he is a regular contributor to the popular BBC Radio 4 programme *The Living World*.

ROBERT A. MORGAN is Nest Records Officer at the BTO. He is a qualified bird ringer and has made special studies of the bird communities of chalk grassland, as well as of raptors and Stone Curlews. He is a frequent lecturer on many aspects of bird study.

DR RAYMOND J. O'CONNOR, Director of the BTO, is a graduate of the Edward Grey Institute for Field Ornithology at Oxford University where he studied nestling development. His recent research has been into the factors controlling bird populations.

PIP AND EVE WILLSON have happily retired to their splendidly designed bird garden at Medmenham in Buckinghamshire where they have experimented widely with bird-feeding devices. Their work in organising the BTO's Garden Bird Feeding Survey for ten winters was recognised in 1980 by the award of the Trust's prestigious Tucker Medal for services to amateur ornithology.

Acknowledgements

Firstly, I offer my grateful thanks to the team of eight who contributed to the text and who allowed me to draw on their hard-won fund of knowledge of garden birds – P.G. Davis, G.H. Gush, the late H.G. Hurrell, C.J. Mead, R.A. Morgan, Dr R.J. O'Connor and Mr and Mrs P. Willson. Invaluable help was given by P.G. Davis and D. Bodenham in restructuring various sections, while R.P. Bowman, W.D. Campbell, Dr R.J.O'Connor, the late N.D. Pullen and R. Spencer kindly read and commented on early drafts of chapters.

Secondly, I applaud the dedicated band of over 700 birdwatchers up and down the country who spent many hundreds of hours during the 1970s counting and observing their birds in true BTO fashion before sending on their findings to the Garden Bird Feeding Survey. Their efforts would not have proved possible without the organisational ability of the late Norman Pullen in the formative winters of the survey, followed by a decade of hard but fruitful work by Pip and Eve Willson.

Thirdly, my appreciation goes to a large group of people who have helped in a multitude of ways. Some have supplied information, allowed their findings to be used, or made helpful comments. These include Dr L.A. Batten, Dr W.R.P. Bourne, the late P.T. Coard, S. Davis, C. Fisher, Dr J.J.M. Flegg, P.F. Goodfellow, D. Goodwin, B. Hawkes, I.H. Leach, Miss C.A. Martin, A. de Miller, A. Roberts, H.P. Sitters, R. Spencer and Dr J.H. van Balen.

Finally, BTO staff colleagues have helped with extracting and processing data and with typing – notably Mrs E. Murray, Mrs M. Benson, R.A. Morgan, R. Hudson, D. Partridge, T. Quartly, Mrs D. Smallwood and Miss C. Hunt. To these, and to others not mentioned individually but who have aided me in other ways, may I extend a very large thank you.

DAVID GLUE

1 Introduction: a garden with birds in mind

Winter is the most important time to look after the birds in your garden, when ice or a covering of deep snow lock up the natural food supplies of species like the Blue Tit, Great Tit, Blackbird, Robin and Chaffinch. During the brief hours of winter daylight they will turn increasingly to man and the bird table for food – in severe weather the killer is hunger, not cold.

The aim of this book is to demonstrate ways in which we can encourage birds into our lives by providing food and shelter in our own gardens, and in doing so gain great pleasure from observing their behaviour at close quarters. To achieve this it is not necessary to own a large mature garden: even if, at first, there do not appear to be sufficient birds to justify elaborate preparations, it is surprising how quickly the word spreads that there are peanuts just around the corner! If the food is supplied regularly local birds will lose little time in finding it, and as the winter advances and food becomes scarce they will be joined by others from further and further afield. And if a really hard spell arrives, with heavy snow or ice covering all the natural food supplies, there is nothing like a flock of regular garden-feeding birds to attract the unusual visitor – who will be just as hungry but rather less experienced in the art of surviving at man's expense. Such visits will probably only be fleeting, but they will invariably be exciting. Most of us have a small plot of ground, or failing that a window sill, and these are sufficient to attract a dozen or so colourful species over the course of a year provided a suitable range of foodstuffs is offered. If the plot can be planted with a berry-bearing shrub or two, or a thick evergreen to provide nesting and roosting sites, so much the better.

Catering and gardening for birds is very much a two-way activity. Enormous satisfaction can be gained from watching the antics of the regular Great Tits and Greenfinches as they vie for the contents of a string of peanuts, or from observing at first hand the emergence into the world of a brood of young Blue Tits. Such pleasures enhance

1

the lives of people of all ages and interests: the busy housewife, the housebound elderly and disabled, our knowledge-thirsty children, and the casual birdwatcher as well as the serious ornithologist.

It is impossible to stress too highly the biological importance of gardens, an importance which will almost certainly increase in the foreseeable future. There are currently some 14.5 million homes in the United Kingdom, and this total is still rising as 37,000 acres (15,000 hectares) or so of agricultural land are devoured annually for the building of houses, roads and factories. The great majority of these homes have some kind of garden, and as gardening is placed in the 'top three' of our recreational pursuits most of them do receive at least some attention and maintenance. Assuming an average modern garden to be about 30 feet by 65 feet (9 by 20 metres), this gives us a total garden area of 670,000 acres (270,000 hectares) – just twice the area covered by our 166 National Nature Reserves in 1980: 330,000 acres (135,000 hectares). Gardens in Britain are an extremely valuable reservoir for wildlife, not simply because of the large area which they cover, but because of the extremely varied range of plants to be found in them.

Perhaps one of the most remarkable things about our birds is the way in which they have adapted to this unusual flora, for a high proportion of the trees and shrubs which we now grow are not British natives. If the seed or fruit is edible the birds will very quickly discover it. But it is not only as a source of rather sophisticated food that birds are attracted to gardens. Tall, thick evergreens make ideal roosting places, and both Greenfinches and Goldfinches make regular use of ornamental conifers as nesting sites, while Long-tailed Tits readily abandon the more usual gorse or hawthorn in favour of the equally prickly berberis.

Our gardens therefore represent one of the richest habitats in Britain, a fact which applies to small town gardens as well as to larger ones in the country. This richness is due largely to the activities of the amateur gardener. It is hoped that this book will enable people to make their gardens more attractive to birds without detracting from either their aesthetic appeal or their productiveness.

There has been an enormous expansion in the horticultural trade since the last world war. Garden centres of varying quality have sprung up like mushrooms: some, where the stock is home produced, are very good, but far too many of them buy in mass-produced plants in a very limited range of varieties in the hope that the inexperienced gardener can be persuaded to accept whatever happens to be in stock. The gardener who knows what he wants will do better to seek out the grower; he may even find that the nursery plant is less expensive.

You can derive great pleasure from getting birds to take food from your hand. Blue Tits will come for peanuts, Chaffinches for seed, and Robins for cheese or mealworms. Patience is required – first toss the food at a distance, then encourage the bird on to your hand, which must not move. But don't hand-feed if domestic or wild predators appear frequently in your garden, as birds become very confiding and vulnerable.

Garden centres and garden shops usually carry a stock of bird tables, bird baths and feeding appliances, and the beginner may find himself confronted with a bewildering array of merchandise. The advice given in this book will help him to purchase sensibly and profitably, so that with a little knowledge and foresight at the planning stage, a potentially limited garden for birds can be transformed into a thriving miniature nature reserve.

Bird foods also are offered for sale today in a multitude of forms, both in shops and in catalogues. Advice is given here on the range of suitable foods, the best methods of presenting them so that as many birds as possible can benefit, and individual preferences should a particular species or group of species merit attention. Water is often a neglected feature in the garden, but is vital for all birds; the book describes the varying needs of different species, the most effective way of providing water for them, and the range of birds most likely to come to drink and bathe.

Bird-gardening activities need not be restricted entirely to the places where we live. Areas around offices and industrial premises often offer exciting opportunities for encouraging birds. Many civic and commercial organisations have funds available for landscaping their premises, but the result is all too often a disappointing array of stark gardens and lifeless ponds.

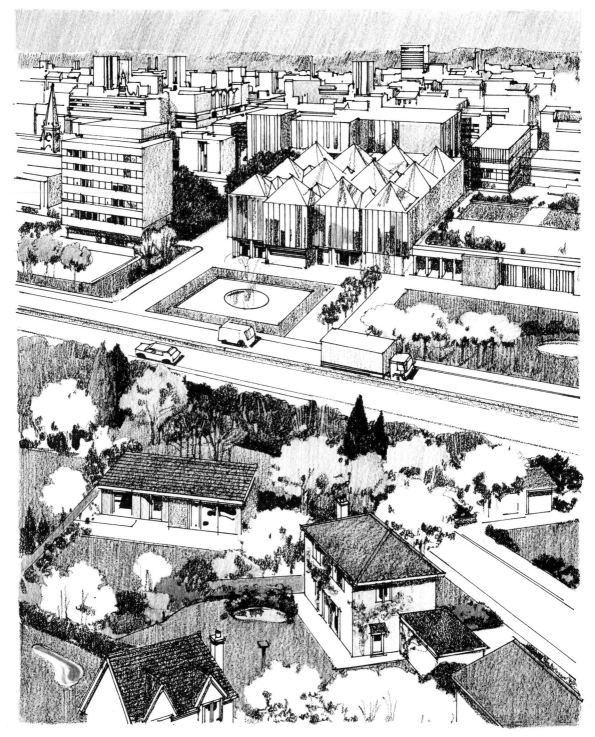

For centuries the British public has been sympathetic towards the needs of our small birds. The tameness of the Robin in this country compared with its Continental counterpart may well have arisen from the woodman's habit of sharing fragments of his picnic. Even in the poverty of the Victorian era people did not forget the needs of their feathered friends. This concern increased in the twentieth century, prompted in post-war years by the BBC, which in times of severe weather followed its news bulletins with requests to provide food and water for the birds.

The practice has undoubtedly spread in recent decades, but the enormous scale of artificial feeding of birds in gardens was not adequately demonstrated until a street survey of over 4000 householders was completed in 1968. Of those questioned one in ten purchased bird food during the course of each winter, over one-third admitted to putting out food regularly, while just over half provided food on a casual basis. Clearly, with a population of some 55 million in Britain, artificial feeding takes place on a very large scale, and every year hundreds of tons of peanuts and seed are put out for the birds.

In an attempt to assess the impact of feeding in gardens on such a scale, the British Trust for Ornithology started a Garden Bird Feeding Survey (the GBFS) in 1970. The facts accumulated over the first decade provide the backbone of this volume. The main aims of the survey have been to determine which species are coming to gardens today and at what times during the year, what range of foods are most often provided by householders and which are the preferred ones.

Suburban (below) and inner city (above) areas offer contrasting possibilities of food and shelter for birds. Note the greater diversity and availability of vegetation adjacent to feeding areas and water in town gardens, although even in the city planners can leave open spaces suitably planted with a range of trees and shrubs.

The sheer size of our native bird population is not widely appreciated, and the bird gardener needs to know that he will have the interests of literally hundreds of mouths in mind if he is contemplating feeding, and scores of birds in the breeding season if he is planning to provide nesting places. An *Atlas of Breeding Birds in Britain and Ireland*, the result of a survey conducted by the BTO and the Irish Wildbird Conservancy during 1968–72, produced some fascinating and valuable clues as to the size of the bird population. The diminutive Wren, with a summer population of some 10 million pairs in peak years, is the most abundant of our birds. The widely distributed Song Thrush, with approximately $3\frac{1}{2}$ million pairs, equates with the number of humans in London, while the Cuckoo population of some 70,000 pairs is comparable with the number of persons in a town the size of Eastbourne. Britain is certainly blessed with a rich diversity and a high density of birds.

Ringing birds for scientific study can be a useful guide to the numbers of birds visiting and feeding. In well stocked gardens a careful watch of the bird table may produce maximum counts of less than a dozen Blue Tits or Greenfinches feeding at any one time during the course of an average winter. The resident ringer, however, may catch, ring and release in excess of 1000 different individuals of each species.

As well as large numbers of the more common birds, one can also expect to attract a wide variety of species into the garden. Although poorly conceived commercial and residential development in some areas is placing a strain on our wildlife, many birds are adapting readily towards a peaceful coexistence with man. During recent decades there have been exciting additions to many gardens situated in built-up, as well as rural, areas. These have included birds like Sparrowhawk, Kestrel, Collared Dove, Tawny Owl, Great Spotted Woodpecker, Blackcap, Siskin, and the trend is certain to continue.

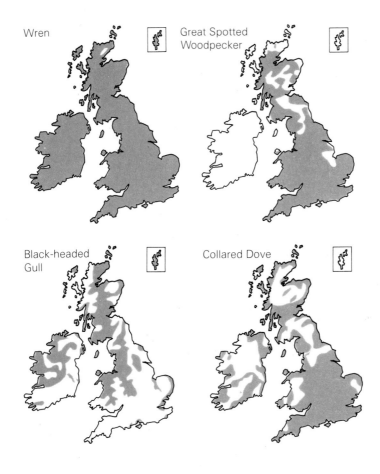

Contrasting breeding distributions of four garden birds. The Wren and Collared Dove are widespread residents, while the Great Spotted Woodpecker and Black-headed Gull are winter visitors to some gardens. Maps taken from the Atlas of Breeding Birds in Britain and Ireland, *compiled from fieldwork completed during 1968–72.*

Record tallies

Few of us can expect to have a garden to match that of Buckingham Palace: the Palace grounds cover 39 acres (16 hectares), are screened by good walls and so get little disturbance, and despite being set in the heart of London, have proved a haven for birds. During investigations in 1960–63, a team of expert naturalists recorded 61 species of birds, 21 of which were found to be nesting. The average bird gardener, however, can expect to attract 15–19 species to take artificially provided food, and to observe 35 species in the garden in the course of an average year, while the sharp-eyed enthusiast will not find it too difficult to push his 'tally' past the 80 mark after regular years of observation to include both birds 'in' and casuals 'flying over'. Keeping a garden tally is an interesting exercise, which has resulted in extremely keen bird-watchers recording as many as 85 species taking food or water and 170 different species being observed inside their garden boundaries. But these are very much the exceptions.

The ethics of feeding our wild birds artificially and helping to increase the numbers of many already common species are often questioned, and merit careful thought. Is it wise? There can be no doubt that even allowing for the occasional outbreaks of disease (which can be eliminated through the correct control measures as shown), deliberate feeding by man does enable more individuals of very many more species to exist than would otherwise be the case. The same, of course, applies to species such as the Black Kite on the Continent, the Red Kite in this country up to the eighteenth century, wild Bewick's Swans on winter wildfowl refuges, Collared Doves, and many other species which may not be deliberately fed by man but scavenge 'waste' or 'steal' food from him.

There may be valid conservation objections to feeding birds if, as seems likely, some of the species thus enabled to maintain abnormally large populations are competing with less abundant species. House Sparrows and Starlings may become 'nest competitors' or 'nest stealers' from Great Tits and Great Spotted Woodpeckers respectively, or the tits, in their turn, may occupy every available nest site so that when the migrant Redstarts and Pied Flycatchers return they are compelled to use quite unsuitable sites which are easily accessible to predators. These problems are not insoluble, and suggestions for coping with them are given throughout the book, but those purists who object to the feeding of birds or the provision of artificial nesting sites on the grounds of 'interfering with nature' may have difficulty in drawing a logical line today. Should all Swallow and House Martin nests in or under the eaves of buildings be destroyed because 'nature intended' these species to breed only where there were suitable caves and overhung cliffs? The *Atlas of Breeding Birds in Britain and Ireland* shows that both species now breed throughout the length of both countries; what it does not show is that probably less than 1 per cent of them nest in 'natural' sites – the rest have to make do with buildings!

On the question of whether we should continue to feed the birds during spring and summer there are two diametrically opposed schools of thought. There are those who condemn the practice entirely, holding that the natural foods which become increasingly plentiful as the days lengthen are far more beneficial to the birds than anything we can provide. On the opposite side are those who believe that it is wrong to encourage the birds to congregate in numbers in and around the garden in the knowledge that food will be forthcoming, and then abruptly to cut off the supply simply because the days are getting longer. A case can be made for both points of view.

There can be no argument that birds need our help during the winter, particularly when the ground is frozen hard or covered in a thick layer of snow so that natural foods are no longer available, but having encouraged a disproportionately large bird population to gather, many of which would not otherwise have remained in the area, it is obviously wrong to cut off the additional supplies of food as soon as the weather improves in the hope that the birds can now find what they need without further assistance. There will be too many of them for this to be possible and they will disperse very reluctantly, having become accustomed to the readily available larder. Dispersal will come later, in early spring for most species, when a large number of the birds will have to go since only a limited number of breeding territories can be accommodated in that area, and it might then appear that artificial feeding could cease; if it were simply a case of obtaining sufficient food for survival this might be the case.

However, it is at this time that for many species 'courtship feeding' commences, when the female may receive up to 70 meals a day from the male. This, in addition to suggesting that the female is in critical need of additional food while forming her eggs, means that the male also has to find a great deal more food and expend considerably more energy than he would otherwise need to do. It seems a strange time to decide that extra feeding is no longer necessary.

The strongest argument against continuing to feed artificially during spring and early summer is that the food which we offer is unsuitable for the young when newly hatched, and if the winter programme of feeding is allowed to continue unchanged at this time the argument is certainly valid. Much depends upon the weather. In a mild spring followed by a warm month of May, when the trees are dripping with the small green caterpillars upon which so many species depend at this time for feeding their young, artificial feeding may not be essential, although in this case it is usually safe to leave the decision to the birds. If there is a glut of caterpillars there will be few visitors to the bird table. If, on the other hand, the spring is cold, or a prolonged drought has inhibited the development of insect

Male and female Robins sport the same plumage and both sexes vigorously defend territories in winter, but it is the cock bird who from late March starts courtship feeding, gathering small insects, spiders and bird table titbits for his mate.

life or kept the earthworms well below the soil surface, some assistance will be welcomed. Many tit and thrush broods in gardens have been seen to survive wet and cold spells of weather when their parents have relied heavily on food scraps from the householder.

A compromise solution seems to be to continue to feed, but to modify the winter programme drastically, and to be guided to some extent by the weather both at the time and during the previous week or ten days. Certain foods should be excluded at this time, for if natural food is scarce the adults cannot be expected to discriminate, and if nestling tits receive an unduly high proportion of bread, hard fat or, even worse, whole peanuts, the results could be fatal.

The end of March is the correct time to make the change; only an occasional Robin, thrush or Blackbird is likely to have newly hatched young before this date, but if this should happen, and the adults are seen to be carrying away food, the bread ration should be discontinued. Most animal fats are safe but they should be presented in such a way that the parents are not able to carry away large lumps. Cheese is good too, but again it should either be grated or put through the mincing machine. Any form of insect food is excellent at this time but the demand for mealworms is always likely to exceed the supply and other forms of live food are rarely available. One solution here is to spend an energetic hour or two digging in the

A well-kept lawn, regularly dug vegetable patch and a compost heap enable parent Song Thrushes to collect ample supplies of earthworms to satisfy their hungry broods. However in cold or drought small quantities of suitable 'supplied' foods will help the birds.

garden; the local thrushes and Robins will certainly approve. Expensive alternatives include softbill food normally given to aviary birds and the meal which poultry keepers offer to newly hatched chicks, but these should only be offered if one's purse allows and the weather demands.

Birds have been adapting to changing conditions for millions of years, and will continue to do so. The difference today is in the time scale, for whereas natural changes take place over hundreds or thousands of years, man-made changes are accomplished almost overnight. Our gardens may be able to absorb some of the species displaced from woodland or farmland, but the plight of those which inhabit the more specialised habitats such as heathland, water meadows or marshland is much more serious. Unless something radical is done soon to prevent the destruction of these habitats it is likely that only the birds that can live with man under artificial conditions, relying partly on his charity and wholly on his tolerance, will survive at all. It is essential that these facts should be publicised as widely as possible, and in particular that the younger generation should be made aware of them. In a household where caring for the birds is a daily, pleasurable duty, a start has already been made.

12

2 Designing a bird garden

Planning your garden

Before settling down to the enjoyable task of designing your garden with birds in mind, it is advisable to consider both your aims and the resources available.

The bird gardener's main aim will be to encourage those species, such as Great Tit and Greenfinch, which already inhabit the surrounding area to visit the garden regularly and in greater numbers than they would otherwise do, and to attract the less usual species like Nuthatch and Siskin by providing facilities – food, shelter, nesting or roosting sites – which are superior to those available elsewhere. This will entail designing an area which may contain sheltered corners that will enable birds to continue to feed even during the most inclement weather, where additional cover will provide roosting sites at all times of the year and nesting sites in spring and summer, where additional rations can be found during the lean months of the year, and where a constant supply of water for drinking and bathing is always available, free from the attention of most mammalian predators.

At first sight the designing of such a garden may appear to be a daunting task, and it is important at this stage to take into account the present state of the garden and the resources, both physical and financial, at your disposal. Much will depend upon the size of the plot, the nature of the area outside the garden, and whether the site is completely bare when you begin. If the garden is on a newly developed estate it may well be nothing more than a flat area of roughly bulldozed mud with a patch or two of weeds, but if the

A shy and retiring bird on the Continent, where it frequents deep woodland, in Britain the Robin appears in most gardens and is popularly voted our national bird. Not long after you have turned over the vegetable patch or compost heap, your garden will almost certainly be visited by an inquisitive Robin seeking earthworms.

13

house has been previously occupied it is almost certain to have some sort of planted cover, in which case decisions will have to be made about what is to be retained or modified and what must be discarded. Anything over half an acre will undoubtedly have vegetation of some description, and it is far better to decide at once what may be of use in the bird garden and to grub out everything else. It is usually easier to start with a clean slate, but this will naturally be more expensive and is in no way imperative.

When starting from scratch the labour and time available, the cost of buying or hiring equipment and the cost of the plants will all have to be considered. Hired labour is expensive, but if there is a considerable amount of heavy work to be done it may be worth while. The preparation of the site for the lawn, the removal of unwanted trees and scrub, the excavation of a pond or any other task where large quantities of soil have to be moved are all operations which can be accomplished more easily and speedily if the necessary equipment is available. It may be possible to hire such equipment, but this too is expensive, and for such tasks it may pay to call in outside assistance.

The cost of a plant depends largely on the amount of time the nurseryman has spent in producing it, and this in turn is an indication of the ease or otherwise with which it can be propagated and the speed of its subsequent growth. Fortunately most of the indispensable shrubs for the bird garden – the cotoneasters, berberis, pyracanthas and aronias – are quite easy to propagate and are, therefore, relatively cheap, but if a large number are required, or if you are a keen gardener and would like to grow your own plants, hints on propagation are given later in the chapter. These easily grown shrubs have the further advantage that they all bear fruit with commendable regularity from a very early age. A seedling cotoneaster, for example, will probably produce a few berries during its third year and from then on the amount will increase annually for many years. Berberis and pyracantha grown from cuttings may even bear a berry or two during their first year of independent life, but the important thing in these early stages is to encourage the plant to form a good framework. Once a sound root system has been achieved growth will be rapid, so it is advisable to get the young plant into its permanent position as soon as possible; nothing is gained by allowing the roots to wander round and round inside a pot or plastic container.

Whether you are starting with a bare site, radically altering an existing garden or thinking of adapting your own well established and much-loved patch there are certain basic requirements which you should consider.

14

The essentials

Trees, or at least one tree even in the tiniest plot, are important because many birds make good use of these as observation posts from which to survey the area in order to satisfy themselves that it is safe to venture further. So if there is a tree in the garden it should be retained; if not, suitable trees can be planted.

Hedges are a necessary feature of the bird garden, both for the benefit of the birds themselves and as a means of excluding the less welcome mammals. Mixed hedges are preferable to the traditional single-species hedges of British gardens: not only do they provide a variety of foods over a long period, they are also useful to the birds as cover and as nesting sites.

Shrubs, particularly the berry-bearing variety, are of great value in the bird garden. Those sited against a wall or fence afford shelter as well as being a source of food supply, and even an unpromising north-facing wall can be enhanced by the brilliant berries of the pyracantha.

Lawns are important to birds. Quite probably most of the neighbouring gardens will have lawns and there may be a park or playing fields nearby; in either case the potential supply of worms and grass-feeding larvae may be adequate, but you still need an open, natural feeding area for the less assertive or less aggressive birds like Song Thrush and Dunnock who will not face the hurly-burly of the feeding table. However, if alternative grassland is available and your space is limited, the lawn need not be very large.

Evergreen trees and shrubs, notably conifers, are useful in the garden since they provide good nesting cover for the first broods of species such as the Chaffinch, Blackbird, Dunnock, seen here, and Wren. In winter they offer safe, sheltered roosting sites.

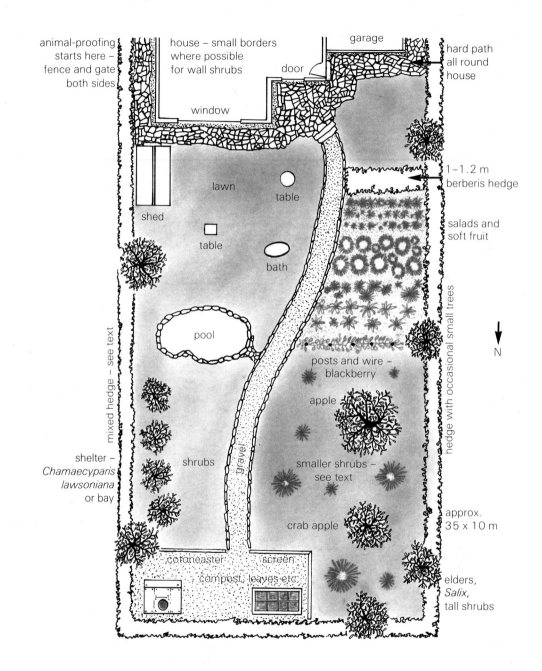

animal-proofing
starts here –
fence and gate
both sides

house – small borders
where possible
for wall shrubs

garage

door

hard path
all round
house

window

lawn

table

1–1.2 m
berberis hedge

shed

table

salads and
soft fruit

bath

pool

posts and wire –
blackberry

N

apple

mixed hedge – see text

hedge with occasional small trees

shelter –
*Chamaecyparis
lawsoniana*
or bay

shrubs

gravel

smaller shrubs –
see text

crab apple

approx.
35 x 10 m

cotoneaster

screen

compost, leaves etc.

elders,
Salix,
tall shrubs

Several species of bird need the protection afforded by low and ground-cover plants. These can be either prostrate, broad-spreading shrubs (there are several good varieties in the versatile cotoneaster family), or plants such as honeysuckle, bryony and guelder rose which have been allowed to ramble in the wilder parts of the garden.

Water is an essential requirement. This can be provided quite adequately in a bird bath or other small container, but depending on the space (and means) available, you may like to think of constructing a pool in your garden.

These are the outlines of what you should hope to provide directly for the birds' benefit. There are one or two other points you should bear in mind when planning your design.

A hard path is essential for the area immediately around the house and along at least one side of the lawn. This will form the access to the feeding ground when the last of the crops in the bird garden are exhausted, and several visits a day to replenish the bird table will be necessary no matter what conditions are like under foot.

One final item calls for our attention: the compost heap, glory hole, dump – call it what you will. Conventional gardeners of the dedicated variety compost everything in order to return the goodness to the soil; bird gardeners know too that good compost is full of worms.

The requirements discussed so far are common to all gardens; it is only the scale of the operation which varies. Obviously a far wider range of food plants can be grown on a two acre site than will be possible in a suburban garden, say 10 metres by 35 metres. The trees in the former can be larger, too. An area of 'wild' ground, where the weeds and brambles are allowed to grow unchecked, can probably be hidden away out of sight of disapproving neighbours in the larger garden, and those species which would not normally be expected to breed in an area surrounded by houses may well do so in unkempt patches at the far end of a garden of this size. It should be clear, therefore, that the final choice will have to be left to the gardener; he alone will know what space is available and where the various lines must be drawn. The most useful plants are discussed in the following pages, and their value (and weaknesses) in the bird garden are presented. A more comprehensive catalogue is given in the table on pp. 202–3, but even this is not exhaustive (see for example the berberis species) and a visit to an autumn show or a walk through a local arboretum may suggest alternative varieties. This is part of the fun of gardening, for fashions change and new varieties come and go.

The garden plan on the left is a working compromise between the ideal garden for birds and a conventional 'acceptable' design. Essential features include a pool and really good visibility from the back window of the house right down the garden, as in the garden overleaf. You can expect to attract most of the birds on pp. 18–19, shown using their favourite feeding and nesting places and song posts, and many more besides.

Chaffinch

Blue Tit

Great
Spotted
Woodpecker

Greenfinch

Blackbird

Song Thrush

Starling

Treecreeper

Robin

Spotted Flycatcher

Dunnock

House Sparrow

Pied Wagtail

Wren

Bullfinch

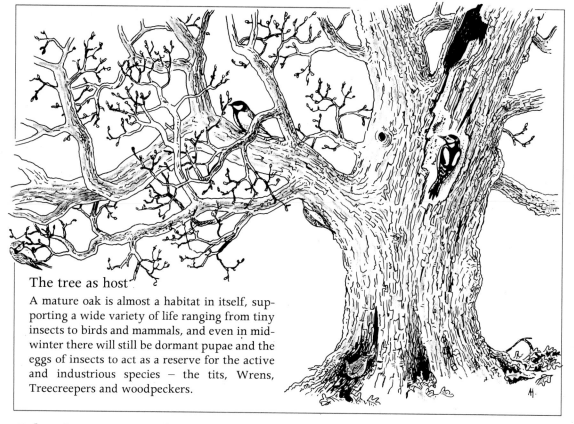

The tree as host

A mature oak is almost a habitat in itself, supporting a wide variety of life ranging from tiny insects to birds and mammals, and even in midwinter there will still be dormant pupae and the eggs of insects to act as a reserve for the active and industrious species – the tits, Wrens, Treecreepers and woodpeckers.

Selecting trees and shrubs

Trees for food and shelter

When choosing trees avoid the forest giants such as oak (*Quercus*), beech (*Fagus*) and ash (*Fraxinus*) in all but large gardens, for sooner or later they will overshadow valuable planting space, their roots will extract far more than their fair share of food and moisture from the soil and they may even, if close to the dwelling, become dangerous. Mutilation, under the banner of 'tree surgery', is usually ugly and at best only a temporary measure. On the other hand a mature tree cannot be replaced in less than forty years (and in many districts if the site has been developed recently it will probably be protected by a Tree Preservation Order). All trees are, of course, of considerable value to birds, and the ideal is to have a tree or trees either outside the garden or on the furthermost boundary: near enough to attract the birds, distant enough to have no adverse effect on subsequent plantings.

In the small bird garden a single carefully chosen tree may suffice. Of the smaller trees rowan (*Sorbus aucuparia*) or, on chalk soils, whitebeam (*S. aria*) both produce a crop of berries at a very early age. Unfortunately in the south of England at least these are quickly snapped up by Blackbirds, Song Thrushes and Mistle Thrushes and frequently by hordes of Starlings, so that by the time the Redwings and Fieldfares arrive there is nothing left. Harvesting part of the crop for use later in the year may be one solution. On a larger site an alder (*Alnus glutinosa*) on a wet spot, or birch (*Betula pubescens*), if the soil is poor and dry, both grow quickly and produce seed which is of value to small finches, especially Redpolls and Siskins. If a garden of more than an acre is completely devoid of trees a larch (*Larix*) or even a group of two or three will remedy the situation as quickly as anything. They too will produce useful seed.

One dual-purpose tree or shrub that should be in every bird garden, no matter how small, is the pussy willow (*Salix caprea*) – not for its seeds but for the teeming insect life which it attracts long before the majority of plants have begun to stir. It is on this tree that we are most likely to record the first bumble bee, the first honey bee, a newly awakened butterfly and a host of gnats and midges which only an expert would attempt to name, and it is these which will induce the early Chiffchaff or Willow Warbler to pause before continuing its spring journey. Goldcrests and all the tits, including the Long-tailed Tit, will join in, but the newly arrived warblers invariably steal the limelight.

If there is an apple tree in the garden it is probably better to store the fruit and ration it out when it is most needed, but the fruit of the crab apple will hang on the tree almost indefinitely and the birds can take it as they need. Somewhat surprisingly it is often the Marsh Tit which begins the onslaught, and he is not interested in the flesh of the apple at all, he wants the pips! All the thrushes will take crab apples, but they are frequently neglected until the weather becomes really severe. Golden Hornet and John Downie are good varieties.

One or two coniferous trees are worth mentioning if only for the shelter which their thick, evergreen foliage affords. For the really small garden needing a tall tree as a song post for a Song Thrush or Blackbird, the cypress *Chamaecyparis lawsoniana columnaris* is hard to beat. It is quick growing, and at 9 or 12 metres high will still be only just over a metre in diameter, so that it occupies very little ground space. Several of the ornamental varieties of *Chamaecyparis* are useful as shelter trees and all provide excellent nesting sites (low down for Dunnocks, higher up for the Goldfinches and Greenfinches) while the tip makes a song post for Chaffinch or Song Thrush. Siskins and Redpolls will often take the seed of the cypress at the end of winter. For the smaller garden *C. lawsoniana* 'Ellwoodii' is about the best.

A hedge for all seasons

The bird garden needs hedges – thick, thorny hedges, clothed to the ground, preferably evergreen, and where possible bearing fruit of some kind which will help to augment the birds' rations during winter. Traditionally hedges in Britain are single-species – such as privet (*Ligustrum*), holly (*Ilex*) and hawthorn (*Crataegus*). Farmland hedges almost invariably comprise the last, interspersed with a few self-sown seedlings of other species. For our purpose mixed hedges are much preferred, for not only do they provide a variety of foods over a long period, they are also useful as cover and as nesting sites. Hawthorn and holly provide a dense thorny growth which will deter the larger mammals, as do pyracantha and berberis. Yew (*Taxus baccata*) makes a thick, twiggy hedge and is useful in shady places, but omit it if the garden abuts farmland or the paddock in which the children's pony grazes, for it is highly poisonous to mammals – the half-wilted trimmings particularly so. A mature yew tree is a most useful acquisition inside the bird garden, for both the berries and the kernels of the seeds within are attractive to a number of birds; clipped yew hedges, however, are unlikely to bear fruit.

To get the best results from hawthorn rather specialised treatment is well worth while for the first few years. The plants should be set out 25–35 cm apart and allowed to grow without check for a year or two until the trunks are about 2.5 cm in diameter at the base. Then during the dormant winter period, they can be 'pleached' as shown opposite.

This job, also known as plashing, laying or layering, may appear complicated but is easier than it sounds. It is one of the dying arts of the countryside – a victim of the tractor-driven hedgecutter which tears and slashes the hedge at a far greater rate than the old countryman could ever hope to compete with. So if there is a retired ancient farmworker in the village, get him to demonstrate; if not, and your first attempt results in a disastrous beheading of the whole plant, don't worry. Six or eight new shoots will soon replace the one you have cut away!

Holly makes a good hedge, but like yew it is unlikely to bear berries if it is clipped regularly, as should be the case. Holly is also rather expensive because it strongly resents root disturbance, so the nurseryman has to give it a lot more attention than other hedging plants. In some areas there may be opportunities to collect wild seedlings salvaged from the leafmould of the woodland floor or from a ditch beneath the trees in which the thrushes congregate after feeding on the berries. These seedlings, pulled out of a thick bed of leafmould, with the whole root intact and encompassed by a mass of half-decaying leaves, can be established with ease; they will frequently outstrip the larger nursery plants which have had their roots damaged or confined for too long in a pot.

So the hedge planting proceeds: a few yards of hawthorn, a couple of *Berberis thunbergii*, a stretch of mixed holly and beech (substitute hornbeam (*Carpinus betulus*) on heavy clay), perhaps a native privet (*Ligustrum vulgare*) to produce the bunches of black berries so popular with Bullfinches – but NOT, please, *Ligustrum ovalifolium*, the privet so often used as a hedging plant, which carries no fruit, bears no thorns and needs clipping at least three times a year if it is to remain respectable. Holly and beech provide a particularly pleasing mixture for a windswept corner, the russet leaves of the beech contrasting with the glossy green of the holly and the whole providing an almost windproof dormitory for roosting birds. A hazel (*Corylus*) might be allowed to grow out of the top of the hedge unpruned to provide nuts for the Nuthatches; then more hawthorn, a pyracantha or two and a different species of berberis.

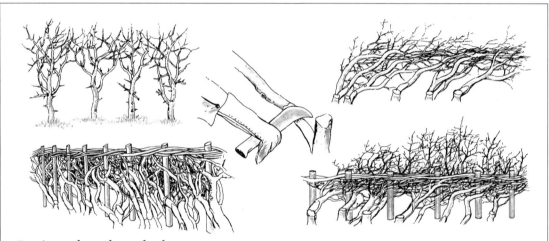

Laying a hawthorn hedge

A cut should be made in the trunk just above ground level and a longitudinal section of the stem about 25 cm long removed above this cut, leaving rather less than half of the main stem attached to the root. If the ground slopes, the cut-away portion should be on the lower side of the plant. When all the plants have been so treated they can be laid on their sides, cut portion uppermost so that the flow of sap is not restricted by tension, and with the main stems a little above horizontal (because sap always flows uphill). The twiggy side-shoots need then to be trimmed back severely, and the layered stems held in position by stakes laid through the prone stems and hammered a few inches into the ground. Almost anything will do for these stakes as they are only needed for a short time. By the time they have decayed, the wounds will have healed and hardened and no further support will be necessary. During the following summer a host of vertical shoots will spring up along the whole length of the near-horizontal stems and the base of the hedge will be as animal-proof as any hedge is likely to be.

Berberis is a huge family of both deciduous and evergreen shrubs – visit a local nursery in September and take note of those which produce the biggest crop of berries, either black or red. If the hedge is long, one or two small trees can be introduced quite easily by allowing a strong shoot to develop unchecked from the top of the hedge, removing the side shoots until the desired length of trunk has been achieved and then allowing it to form a head. Such a miniature tree will produce more berries than several yards of hedge of the same species.

Once planted, the hedge will need little attention apart from an annual trimming. In the early years it is essential to keep the base of the hedge free from rank grass and weeds which would smother the lower branches and result in holes and gaps at the most important level – that at which mammalian predators will attempt to enter. The ultimate height is a matter of choice, but a minimum of two metres for hedges beside public highways or neighbouring gardens will ensure that the birds are not constantly disturbed by passers-by. Whatever the final height, the hedge should be lightly trimmed every year until the desired height is attained, and the sides should always taper in slightly towards the top to allow the rain to reach the foliage at the base.

Plants for the wall

Good use should be made of any available wall space on the house, garage, garden shed or any wooden fence which is to be retained. Before any planting takes place it is advisable to drill holes in the area to be covered, put in stout wall nails and run parallel wires at intervals across the walls. Nothing is worse than having to tie up a wind-blown creeper, particularly if it has a Blackbird or Spotted Flycatcher nesting in it.

A few plants, like wisteria (*Wisteria sinensis*) are natural climbers and have a tendency to twine round any available support. Once established, these climbers need little attention beyond trimming back when the plant has reached the limit of its allotted space (see p. 39). The gardener traditionally uses several plants as wall shrubs which are not natural climbers and for those certain training is necessary.

Pyracantha is probably the shrub most frequently found clothing a high wall facing either north or east for the simple reason that it is one of the few plants which will grow, flower and fruit abundantly in a situation which the majority of climbers would not tolerate. It is, therefore, an indispensable subject for the bird garden, but the treatment of individual plants must vary according to the site in which they are planted and the job they are expected to

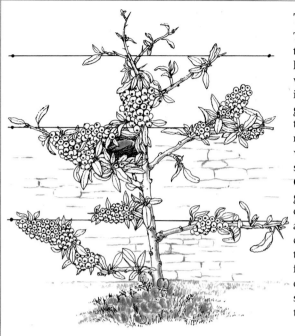

Training a pyracantha

The leading shoot – the growing tip – should be tied in as it develops and the strongest of the lateral shoots tied to the horizontal wires. This will form the framework of the plant. Tying in is easy so long as it is undertaken while the growths are young and green, for at this stage they may be bent through ninety degrees or more; if there is a vacant wire with no convenient shoot to occupy it, the nearest available shoot can be bent round and firmly tied in. Once the wood has hardened it will continue to grow in that direction for the rest of its life. All other shoots should then be cut back to within about 20 cm of the framework; this should be done annually when the rest of the climbers are trimmed. These shortened branches will soon form knotty spurs very like the fruiting spurs on an old apple tree – spurs which are ideal for supporting and hiding nests – and will continue to bear fruit just as they do on the apple trees.

perform. An occasional pyracantha can be included in the hedge, where it will be clipped along with its neighbours, although in this case the quantity of berries will naturally be reduced. On a wall the pyracantha will need to be controlled, for it is by nature a shrub and not a climber at all. For this the stout wall nails and wires are essential (see above).

Pyracantha atalantioides, sometimes listed as *P. gibbsii*, will grow up to 6 metres, has brilliant red berries which frequently hang until well after Christmas before the birds become interested, and is absolutely hardy in the bleakest of positions. Others are *P.* 'Orange Glow', with orange fruit, and *P. rogersiana* 'Flava', yellow. It would be interesting to plant all three on the same wall to discover which are taken first, for there is a theory among nurserymen and the writers of horticultural journals that the 'coloured' berries (i.e. yellow, orange, pink or white) are less attractive to birds. Could this be that the young birds are accustomed to the red berries of earlier fruiting trees such as hawthorn (*Crataegus monogyna*) and rowan? Despite the pronouncements of the horticultural pundits there will be few berries of any colour left on the pyracantha, no matter what their colour, by February.

If there is still a vacant space on a north wall, *Garrya elliptica* provides marvellous nest sites for early broods of Blackbird and

Song Thrush. It has no food value, but the dark, evergreen leaves form a dense screen and the foot-long, jade green catkins smother the plant from mid-January onwards. For lower walls and for the narrow borders beneath windows *Mahonia japonica* (once called *M. bealei*) will produce purple-black bunches of berries which are usually taken very early in the season, in July and August. This is a shrub, not a climber, but the protection afforded by a wall will be much to the plant's liking.

North walls are the most difficult to clothe, but the plants mentioned above will grow and thrive on a wall which receives no sun at all. The sunnier, warmer sites will support climbers which would fail in less congenial sites so we plant up the north and east walls first, leaving those facing west or south for the plants which insist on sunshine for at least part of the day. Here the choice is much wider. Any of the honeysuckles (*Lonicera* species) will do well, but probably none of the cultivated varieties outshines our native *L. periclymenum* for scent or in the production of berries which are sought after by Marsh Tits, Blackcaps and occasionally Bullfinches. *L. henryi* is also useful; it has the added advantage of being evergreen and where growth is vigorous will support the nests of birds from Wren to Collared Dove in size.

An essential plant for any wall covering operation is *Cotoneaster horizontalis*. It requires a minimum of training, the herringbone branches grow flat against the support and every twig is smothered in glowing red berries. Occasionally, perhaps if it is growing in a rather inaccessible place beneath a window, the berries may be neglected until around Christmas, but many a birdwatcher has seen his first Waxwing feeding on these berries or on those of the pyracantha.

Ivy (*Hedera helix*) is often frowned upon in the garden but it is a valuable climber if its growth is checked regularly. The flowers, produced late in the year, attract swarms of insects, and the foliage and stems harbour dormant insects and larvae in winter. It is a great asset for roosting birds and gives suitable nest sites for birds like the Goldcrest, while the berries in spring are taken regularly by thrushes, Woodpigeons, Blackcaps and others.

If you live in the southern half of England, it is well worth trying a vine. *Vitis heterophylla* is a vigorous climber with distinctive, dainty foliage; when established it produces profuse clusters of turquoise grapes, and even if the local Blackbirds have never seen anything quite like this before they very quickly learn. *Vitis* 'Brandt' is another excellent vine, but here the difficulty is that the bird gardener's family will probably find the fruit as attractive as do the Blackbirds and thrushes!

Cotoneasters are invaluable in the garden, since the berries are available after those of the rowan have been eaten and before the ivy fruits ripen. The masses of coral red berries produced by Cotoneaster horizontalis *are a favourite food of the Fieldfare, one of our most attractive winter visitors from Scandinavia.*

Several other culinary fruits are very satisfactory when trained against a wall. Red and white currants can be grown in this way, as well as blackberries; in the latter case the thornless varieties are recommended since the old canes must be removed every year. Against a low wall the Japanese wineberry (*Rubus phoenicolasius*) is both attractive and prolific in the production of clusters of amber berries.

Further useful berry-bearing shrubs

A number of berry-bearing shrubs might be called dual-purpose plants. If there is space available they can be allowed to throw up a number of strong branches from ground level and eventually a bush perhaps six metres high and the same across will result. Alternatively, with judicious pruning in the early stages this same plant can be persuaded to form a small tree with a single trunk, ideal for

27

a small garden. All that is required is the gradual – and it must be gradual – removal of all but one of the shoots at ground level. Once all the sap is being channelled into a single stem, growth will be rapid and the main stem will produce side shoots; these too should be pinched out, again gradually, until a bare 'trunk' of the required height is reached, when any further side shoots can be permitted to remain and the crown of the tree will be formed.

Elder (*Sambucus nigra*), probably the most useful berry-bearing shrub of all, since everything from a Woodpigeon down to a Chiffchaff will eat the fruit, can be treated in this way; so can hawthorn and hazel – cob nuts and filberts offered in catalogues are only sophisticated hazels. The same applies to the evergreen *Stranvaesia davidiana*, a most useful plant to have in the bird garden because the fruit ripens slowly and the birds do not become interested until very late in the year, at which time the Scandinavian thrushes may manage to get their share. Three good cotoneasters are *C. bullatus*, *C. frigidus* and *C. watereri*, all of which will grow either as large shrubs or as small trees. *C. bullatus* is very popular with the thrush family and it has the unusual property of fruiting over a long period, so that green berries are still developing when the first flush of ripened fruit is being consumed.

These pages show berry-bearing garden shrubs and trees which provide a valuable source of food for birds at different times of year – above, left to right and top to bottom: rowan, whitebeam, privet, holly, pyracantha and yew.

Above, left to right and top to bottom: Berberis darwinii, *honeysuckle,* Cotoneaster horizontalis, Cotoneaster bullatus, *elder and purging buckthorn.*

Some berries appear to be more palatable than others; the birds will clear one hawthorn completely before starting on another which appears to be identical or, given a choice of three rowans in the same garden, will invariably take them in the same order each year. So when nurserymen tell us that birds are not attracted to the fruit of *Cotoneaster frigidus* and *C. watereri* they may be right. Certainly these berries can often be seen on the trees well after Christmas. In the bird garden this can be a decided advantage, since if all berries were equally attractive there can be little doubt that few would be left by the time the really hard weather arrived. They will be taken eventually, and again it may be that some of the scarcer visitors to the garden – a Waxwing perhaps – will benefit.

Low-lying shrubs

In choosing shrubs to provide much needed ground cover for the birds, we shall once again be leaning heavily on the two indispensable families, berberis and cotoneaster, and in case the reader's reaction is 'not again' a glance at the illustrations above will make it clear that the species within these families are absolutely distinct. So if constant repetition of the names becomes a little wearisome, at least the plants are not.

29

Berberis is the classic example of a family where it pays to visit a nursery and choose the plant to suit the site for which it is required, for the number of species and varieties in cultivation make it impossible for any nursery to grow them all, and good substitutes for those which are suggested here will almost certainly be available. One which should be in every garden is *B. darwinii*, beautiful in flower, foliage and fruit, while *B. gagnepainii* and *B. wilsonae* both produce heavy crops of berries. The first two are evergreen, the third deciduous. Closely related to these is *Mahonia japonica* which bears long chains of purple berries. The aronias are suckering shrubs rarely exceeding 1.5 metres; all are good, with *A. melanocarpa* probably the best of all.

Most of the laurels are far too large for the average garden by the time they have reached fruiting age, but the recently introduced *Prunus laurocerasus* 'Otto Luyken' forms a low, compact shrub of about 1 metre with narrow, shining green leaves and white 'candles' followed by huge black berries which are eagerly taken by the thrushes. Another unusual shrub is *Coriaria terminalis xanthocarpa*, a suckering sub-shrub bearing foot-long chains of amber berries.

Berries form an important part of the winter diet of members of the thrush family including Blackbirds.

Treat this like a raspberry, cutting down all the old canes at the
end of the year. Horticultural works tell us that birds do not eat
the berries, but Whitethroats and Blackcaps, as well as the thrush
family, do not read horticultural works and they seem none the
worse for that.

It takes many years for a holly to bear significant quantities of
fruit so we include it with the smaller growing subjects. Here the
choice of variety is important, for the holly is dioecious – that is the
male and female flowers grow on different plants – and the chance
of getting a good berry-bearing plant from a bundle of hedging
hollies is indeed small. The golden variegated specimens are
excellent, but care is needed in choosing them: many years ago
someone committed a horticultural howler which has never been
rectified, and the female plant is still called Golden King and the male
Golden Queen. Golden King is the one you want, and it is not usually
necessary to provide a male plant – the hollies in the hedge or in
neighbouring gardens will be sufficient.

Blackberries (*Rubus fruticosus*) are a problem. For some reason
members of the thrush family are not very keen on them and although
many of the warblers will take one or two, many more will be
allowed to shrivel and hang on the bushes until well into winter. In
this state Bullfinches will take them for the seed which they contain.
Brambles should be encouraged to grow in the wild part of the larger
garden where they can associate with the elder, the willows, a clump
or two of raspberries, nettles (*Urtica*) and anything else which sows
itself there. It is a good idea to toss in a dead branch or two when the
patch is developing; the brambles will soon cover these and they will
form excellent nesting places for Blackcap, Garden Warbler or
Whitethroat. In the small garden it is probably better to be content
with one of the thornless blackberries (see p. 27).

Further native shrubs

One or two other native shrubs may be included if they are available.
Both the purging buckthorn (*Rhamnus cathartica*) and the alder
buckthorn (*Frangula alnus*) produce black fruit which is readily
taken, and have the additional merit that their leaves are the food
plant of the brimstone butterfly. *Daphne mezereum*, a rare native but
a common garden plant, may be used in two ways by the birds;
either the fruit-eaters will swallow the berries whole, or Greenfinches will discard the flesh to get at the seed within. The rarer
evergreen daphnes are equally attractive. Dogwood (*Cornus
sanguinea*) might also be included, and the cornelian cherry (*Cornus
mas*), although this can scarcely be recommended for the impatient
gardener since it may take up to twenty years before the first fruit

appears. On chalk soils the wayfaring tree (*Viburnum lantana*) will produce flat heads of berries, at first red but becoming black, and the closely related guelder rose (*V. opulus*) is even more generous with its masses of clear, translucent red fruit. However, these do seem to be somewhat unpalatable; they are frequently allowed to shrivel on the bush and the current year's crop and the withered remains from the previous year can often be found hanging together.

Plants for seaside gardens

Before leaving the subject of planting, the rather specialised methods necessary for dealing with a seaside garden should be mentioned, for here the strong salt-laden winds are not to the liking of some of the shrubs one might otherwise use. Where there is absolutely no protection from these winds, any sort of screen – even wattle hurdles – will help until a living screen can be established, and in this case you do not have to worry about omitting trees which might ultimately become too large; the wind will see that they don't.

Whatever plants are chosen (see below), the exhausted migrants will bless the gardener for the shelter afforded, even if it is not berry laden. Once an outer screen has become established the choice of shrubs which can be grown is almost unlimited, for the climatic influence of the sea is favourable to many plants which would be considered doubtfully hardy further inland. Firm planting and adequate staking are essential under these windswept conditions, and the plants selected for the exposed screen should be smaller than one might normally choose.

Forming a rampart

For a frontal rampart against the wind the pines *Pinus pinaster* and *P. radiata* are sufficiently tough; sycamore (*Acer pseudoplatanus*) is useful in the front line and so are the wild pear (*Pyrus communis*), the Swedish whitebeam (*Sorbus intermedia*) and most of the *Crataegus* species. The holm oak (*Quercus ilex*) is evergreen and so doubly valuable. Tamarisk (*Tamarix gallica*) will flourish here and so will sea buckthorn (*Hippophaë rhamnoides*), and in milder areas the escallonias usually succeed.

Other plants of use to birds

Most of the shrubs already mentioned produce generous quantities of fruit which will attract the flock-feeding species – Starlings and the thrush family – but there are a number of other plants producing much smaller amounts of berries which, although unworthy of the attentions of the flock feeders, are nevertheless of great benefit to individual birds. For over forty years W. D. Campbell conducted a series of experiments in Oxfordshire using various baits to trap birds for ringing, with rather surprising results. Whitethroats and Song Thrushes are attracted to wild arum (*Arum maculatum*); most of the warblers, Robins, Marsh Tits and even Wrens and Dunnocks take the berries of the prostrate evergreen honeysuckle (*Lonicera pileata*). The fruit of woody and deadly nightshade (*Solanum dulcamara* and *Atropa belladonna*), white bryony (*Bryonia dioica*) and black bryony (*Tamus communis*) – four plants whose poisonous properties were constantly impressed upon us as children – are all eaten with relish; and perhaps most surprising of all, Spotted Flycatchers take the berries of honeysuckle, redcurrant, elder, yew and guelder rose. Most of these have one thing in common: they are rather low-growing, and therefore more likely to be discovered by those species which feed mainly in scrub or amongst the undergrowth. It would seem sensible therefore to retain any or all of them if they are already growing in the garden, or to introduce them if they are not – although one might perhaps hesitate before introducing the true deadly nightshade.

Catering for both occasional and regular fruit- and berry-eating species is relatively easy, for although our offerings have been introduced into British gardens from almost every temperate corner of the world they are accepted without question by the birds. It is strange, therefore, that the finches do not seem to have accepted the seeds of some of the introduced annuals and perennials in a similar way. This may be because, like the thrushes, most finches are flock-feeders, only interested in extensive areas of a single plant species – for example, the weeds in a neglected root field. A few of the composites – the 'daisy-flowered' plants – are sought after by Gold-finches; the Mexican aster (*Cosmos* species) and the annual corn-flower (*Centaurea cyanus*) are particularly popular. During hard weather the finches will also investigate the decaying seed heads of Michaelmas daisies (*Aster*), golden rod (*Solidago*) and other daisy-like plants, but the amount of seed they get from these is probably rather small. The giant sunflower (*Helianthus*) is a difficult plant to place in a garden – it always appears to be rather out of proportion – but perhaps a row in the kitchen garden or against the wall of the garden shed might be possible, for the seeds are taken by all the tits,

Nuthatches, Greenfinches, even Hawfinches, and although the dried seeds can be purchased from the corn chandler it is much more interesting to see the birds working for their living.

The seeds of the pansy (*Viola* species), snapdragon (*Antirrhinum*), forget-me-not (*Myosotis*) and wallflower *(Cheiranthus)* are all taken occasionally, usually by Bullfinches, but rarely with any great enthusiasm, and the same could be said of most garden weeds; there are never enough of them to attract large numbers of birds. It is obviously impossible to produce these in a garden on a scale large enough to attract the huge flocks of finches that can be found on a weedy root field during winter, when the plant species are usually redshank (*Polygonum persicaria*), knotgrass (*Polygonum aviculare*) or 'Fat Hen' (*Chenopodium album*), but if the early crops in the kitchen garden are cleared in June there is still time for a few weeds to germinate and mature before the winter, and the local Dunnocks and Chaffinches will make good use of them when times are hard. It is a good plan to leave a few plants of lettuce when the clearing is taking place, allowing them to go to seed. All finches are extremely fond of lettuce seed.

The odd dandelion (*Taraxacum officinale*) or greater plantain (*Plantago major*) growing in the gravel path might be spared for the same reason. Knapweed (*Centaurea nigra*), beloved of Goldfinches, is not a troublesome weed so room might be found for a patch in the

Finches are very adept at spotting localised food sources, and a charm of Goldfinches will be quick to find a small clump of thistles or other seed heads. Only occasionally do they turn to artificially provided foods, although they are regular visitors at garden bird baths or ponds.

wild garden or beneath the orchard trees, and a patch of teasel (*Dipsacus fullonum*) should be included for the same delightful species. If there is a damp area a clump or two of meadowsweet (*Filipendula ulmaria*) would certainly attract Bullfinches and possibly a Redpoll or a Siskin. Now that weedkillers have almost eradicated the larger and more handsome thistles from our fields one might be tempted to grow a specimen or two in the herbaceous border, if only to re-populate some of the waste ground in the neighbourhood.

Other requirements for the bird garden

Making a lawn

Lawns are an important feature of the bird garden but one that will require regular attention during the growing season. As already mentioned in the introduction to this chapter there is no need for the lawn to be a large one, particularly if there is plenty of alternative grassland nearby. Since the lawn provides an essential feeding ground for some of the shyer species, having it within sight of a window is a bonus for the birdwatcher.

Whether seed or turves are used will depend on the urgency of the operation and the depth of the gardener's pocket, but in either case thorough preparation of the site is essential. The best periods for sowing lawn seed are early September, when the ground is warm – but not, of course, during a heatwave when the surface is bone dry – or from late March to mid-May according to the geographical location of the garden. Subsequent treatment for both turf and seed consists of regular mowing, with the cutter set high for the first few cuts and with the grass box left off occasionally to encourage the worms to drag a little humus back into the soil.

Turf or seed?

Turf is more expensive but achieves a quicker result, and if the turf was cut from a field with soil similar to that of the garden then there should be no problems. Seed is cheaper, takes a little longer to establish, and may suffer in the early stages – from birds! House Sparrows and Chaffinches are the worst offenders, but a few strands of black cotton stretched across the lawn should be sufficient to discourage them for the ten days or so during which germination is taking place, and in this case the bird gardener may feel justified in taking a few precautions.

Paths

Access to the various parts of the garden merits careful consideration. As already pointed out, a hard path is necessary round the house and along at least one side of the lawn to provide access to the feeding stations in bad weather. Stone slabs, bricks set on edge or concrete paving slabs will all serve the purpose, and the last need not be unattractive. An imitation stone slab closely resembling York stone is on the market and should be acceptable to all but the purist – or the very wealthy. The resident Song Thrushes may well use the hard surfaces as their 'anvils' on which to smash open a favourite food, the common snail.

Less frequently used paths to the furthermost parts of the garden can be of gravel or, if the garden is particularly large, of grass. The gravel should not be kept scrupulously weed-free, for along the edges and in the cracks and crannies annual meadow grass (*Poa annua*) will undoubtedly appear and this, although its praises often go unsung, is a very important food item in winter. It will germinate during a mild spell even in January, and the interval between germination and seeding is a mere six weeks so that supplies are constantly being replenished. All the finches will take it; Dunnocks also, and Meadow Pipits and wagtails when better things are not available. Close examination of the seed heads of this grass in early spring will reveal too that it is about the earliest of all plants to be attacked by aphids, and insect food of any kind will be acceptable to birds at this time of the year. In the larger garden, grass paths and areas of grass beneath fruit trees should be kept reasonably short, although the weekly mowing given to the lawn is not necessary for them. Long grass is almost completely ignored by birds.

The compost heap

The generous supply of worms that will be present in good compost is largely unavailable to the birds until the heap is broken up and spread around the garden. This is therefore a job to be tackled in winter when there is a little frost in the ground so that the barrow can be wheeled even on to newly dug plots without cutting up the surface and creating a sea of mud. The top layer of the heap will probably be frozen too, but this is of no consequence; the larger lumps will quickly be broken up by the thrushes and Blackbirds when the thaw comes, in their efforts to get at the few worms which remained hidden when the heap was spread. Any which escape will help to build up the worm population around the garden.

The site for the compost heaps should be a remote corner of the garden, tucked away between a screen of shrubs and the hedge. Two heaps are necessary: one in current use while the other is rotting

If the roots of a purchased plant are matted together in a tight ball, soak them in a bucket of water to loosen them; dig a hole larger than the root ball, loosen the bottom of the hole with a fork and, if you have it, mix in a forkful of compost or manure at the same time. A little peat added to the soil when filling in the hole will help to keep it moist while the new roots are developing, and a thorough soaking after planting will settle the soil around them.

down and awaiting spreading. Any vegetable matter is acceptable apart from seeding weeds and the roots of couch grass, docks, nettles and other tough subjects; grass mowings are excellent for providing heat to hasten the process of decay. Household vegetable waste can be added, also scraps of woollen rag and even paper so long as excessive quantities of newsprint and all glossy magazines are excluded. Metal, glass or plastic materials should also be avoided. An occasional layer of animal manure will greatly improve the quality of the final product.

In the small garden autumn leaves can go on the compost heap, but if larger quantities abound they are best stacked separately, last year's half-decayed crop being spread thick around the shrubs in early autumn so that the bin is empty in time to receive the present year's crop. The half-rotted leaves will be a happy hunting ground for birds during the winter.

Where space allows, a wild corner planted up with some native shrubs, including clumps of bramble and nettle, will increase the variety of breeding birds. With luck, a pair of summer migrants such as Whitethroat, Blackcap or even Garden Warbler, seen here, may be tempted to stay and nest.

37

Maintaining the bird garden

The type of garden described so far requires the minimum of maintenance. A few jobs however are essential. Regular mowing, spreading the compost, a little gentle pruning either to control the shape of the developing trees or shrubs or to prevent the more rampant species from encroaching on the area occupied by their equally desirable neighbours, autumn leaf sweeping and periodical tidying up are all tasks which are necessary in any garden. Many birdlovers are also keen gardeners who can be relied upon to find their own ways of satisfying the gardening urge, and the fact that there has been no mention of the vegetable patch, the rose garden or your own favourite plants does not mean that they should be excluded.

Neither planting nor pruning should present problems in our garden. None of the plants suggested is at all temperamental, and all should flourish in any reasonable garden soil. October and November, when the leaves of the deciduous plants have fallen, is the best time for planting but many firms now concentrate on 'container grown' stock which, they assure us, 'can be planted at any time'. If the plants offered have a mass of roots growing through the container, refuse them; what roots there are within the pot will be old and incapable of forming a decent root system. Get open-ground plants whenever possible. March is also a good planting month, especially for evergreens and conifers.

As far as possible pruning, except for a specific purpose, is best avoided. If a pyracantha is to succeed on a wall the pruning which has already been described (see p. 25) is essential; the same plant growing as part of the hedge will be clipped with the rest of the hedge, but if it is allowed to grow naturally, as a shrub in the open garden, no pruning is necessary. When the garden has been established for several years and the shrubs are flourishing some of the stronger growing subjects may tend to subdue their weaker neighbours and a branch or two may have to be removed to let in the light, but systematic annual pruning will only result in a reduction of the berry crop.

However, in the very small garden there just is not the space to allow everything to develop as nature intended, and a method of controlling the size of the plant must be adopted. One which has proved successful is shown opposite.

Increasing your stock

Shrubs are expensive, and the gardener faced with the problem of planting a large area may decide that he would like to grow some of them for himself. Many of the subjects for the bird garden can be

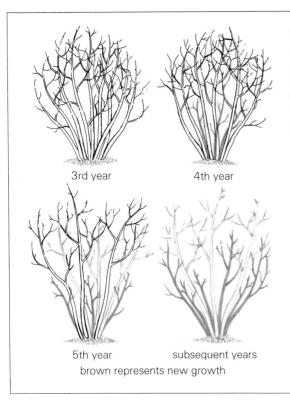

3rd year

4th year

5th year

subsequent years

brown represents new growth

Keeping a shrub within bounds

Let the plant grow to the desired height; then, in autumn, remove one-third of the shoots entirely. During the following summer several new shoots will emerge at ground level and in the following autumn you should repeat the process, taking out a further third of the old shoots. Again the plant will produce new shoots and by the following autumn it will consist of one-third current year's growth, one-third two year old growth and one-third of the original, old growth, which is again cut away. By next autumn you will have a plant with nothing older than three years, old enough to fruit but still of a modest size, and if the process is repeated annually the plant will never get any bigger. These instructions do not have to be rigidly adhered to, of course. If new growth is poor following a hot, dry summer the amount of wood removed can be reduced; if the available space will take a slightly larger shrub, a four year cycle taking out a quarter of the branches each year can be substituted, but the principle remains the same.

produced quite easily and they will bear fruit at a reasonably early age. Seed, of course, is nature's most important way of securing the increase of a species, and in many cases the coloured outer covering of a fruit or berry is simply a device to persuade a bird or an animal to eat it and dispose of the indigestible seed inside at some distance from the parent plant. Unfortunately the seed from many of the berry-bearing shrubs takes two seasons to germinate; the outer casing of a cherry 'stone', for example, is extremely hard, and until the gradual process of decay has weakened it germination cannot take place. Fruit of this sort should be gathered when ripe and stored until spring in slightly damp sand. The open containers are best buried in the ground for the winter but care is necessary to protect the contents from small rodents. If the seed is sown in March, either in boxes or in open ground, a few may germinate immediately, but to obtain a really satisfactory germination this process, called stratification, should continue for a full year.

When the garden has been established for a year or two and the shrubs are beginning to bear fruit in ever-increasing quantities, self-sown (or bird-sown) seedlings will be found appearing in all sorts of odd places. Leave them, if possible, for a plant never grows better than when it has chosen its own habitat. If they become too numerous, however, take them up and plant them in the wild garden or in the vacant spaces between existing shrubs, or give them to your friends so that they too can grow food for the birds.

Taking cuttings

Cuttings will produce a plant more rapidly, and many of the shrubs most useful in the bird garden can be increased in this way. Hardwood cuttings may be taken in the way described below but berberis, pyracantha, cotoneaster – indeed most garden shrubs – are better rooted in pots either in a cold frame or on the kitchen window sill. One of the most reliable methods where only a few plants are needed is the double pot method (see opposite). The best rooting compost is a mixture of sharp sand, peat and loam (or decent garden soil) in the proportions 3:1:1.

Cuttings taken in July, when the growth is still somewhat sappy, root quickly; taken in September or October when the growth is

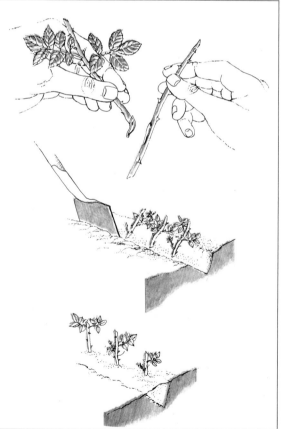

How to succeed with cuttings

Cuttings of elder, wild rose (*Rosa canina*) or willow can be taken during November or December when the tree is dormant. A straight, healthy twig of the current year's growth is pulled off with a downward motion so that it takes with it a little of the wood and the bark of the branch to which it was attached. This heel, as it is called, is carefully trimmed with a sharp knife until a smooth surface is achieved, taking care not to expose the pith – the inner core – of the cutting itself. The cutting is then shortened from the tip to about 25–30 cm and is ready to go into the ground. If only one or two plants of a particular species are required these hardwood cuttings can go straight into their permanent positions in the garden; for larger quantities a row of them in a corner of the garden is better. A V-shaped trench is made by inserting a spade into the ground and rocking it backwards and forwards. The trench is then liberally lined with sharp sand, the cuttings inserted to about half their length and the sides of the trench closed by treading along both edges. For a permanent site three cuttings in a single spade cut should be sufficient. Probably all will root, in which case the weaker ones can be removed during the following summer.

harder they are equally satisfactory but must be left in the pot over winter, so that rooting takes rather longer. In both cases side shoots of the current season's growth about 7–12 cm long are best. The lower leaves which would come into contact with the soil are removed and the heels prepared in the manner already described; a razor blade is an excellent tool for trimming these softer cuttings. About 5 cm of the stem goes into the compost, and the cuttings can be inserted quite close together. A dozen or more in a 15 cm pot is quite usual. If a shaded cold frame is available the pot can stand in this; if not, place the whole unit in a plastic bag, tie up the mouth and place it on the kitchen window sill. A close, humid atmosphere is required and the cuttings must never be allowed to flag.

For cuttings taken in July rooting should be well advanced in about four weeks, and one great advantage of this method is that progress can be ascertained by carefully removing the inner pot without disturbing the plants. If several different species are in the same unit they may not all root equally quickly, but again those which have rooted can be carefully peeled away leaving the remainder to root in their own good time. Watering, apart from the initial soak when the cuttings are inserted, should not be necessary particularly if the plastic bag is used, but if the pot appears dry during a hot spell the inner pot should be filled with water and allowed to drain. The rooted cuttings are best planted singly in pots for their first growing season but if this is not possible they will do quite well planted 15 cm apart in a shady nursery bed. A July rooted cutting should be ready to go into its permanent quarters in the autumn fifteen months later.

When plants such as aronia and coriaria have become well established, suckers will appear around the parent plant. These can be removed in October and either planted in a new site or allowed to grow on for a season in the nursery bed.

Above: Two earthenware (NOT plastic) pots of different sizes are chosen so that when one is placed inside the other there is a gap of about 2 cm between the two. Drainage crocks are placed in the larger pot, together with a little rooting mixture, until the rims of the two pots are level when the smaller pot is inserted. The space between the two pots is then filled with the compost, watered, and allowed to settle while the cuttings are prepared.

Constructing a pond

Water is the one essential item which has not yet been considered; it is by no means the least important. Whether you decide to construct a garden pool will depend once again to some extent on the space and means at your disposal. A pool is a pleasant thing to have, and if it is situated in a quiet spot away from the house it will be used by those species which have not yet the courage to visit the feeding area on the lawn.

If such a pool is planned it is most important that the edges slope very gradually from shallow water to dry land on all sides. There must be no steep walls. For this reason the moulded fibreglass ponds

41

available from garden centres should generally be avoided, for a wet bird, particularly a recently fledged youngster, may flap its way to the edge, but if this is not negotiable it will not turn around and seek a better way out. Polythene cannot be recommended for a permanent pool; butyl rubber sheeting is better, but concrete is worth while if permanence is the ultimate aim.

The early steps in construction are the same in both cases. The shape is marked out with pegs and the ground excavated to the required depth. If you contemplate having water lilies or fish, a depth of 50–60 cm at the centre will be necessary to protect them when the upper layer becomes frozen. If marginal plants are planned

it is necessary to have shelves around the periphery to take a depth of 15–20 cm of soil. In this case allowance must also be made for 10 cm of concrete and 4–5 cm of cement rendering. The shelves are separated from the open water by a perforated concrete wall – a few short lengths of hosepipe let into the walls during construction will suffice – so that the water may seep through and the soil around the water's edge will always be damp. One advantage of such shelves in a pool is that depressions may be excavated on them and these hollows, lined with gravel or pebbles, make excellent bathing places for the birds. Nevertheless the first 30–45 cm of open water should still be kept very shallow.

The concrete mixture is one part cement, three parts washed sand and three parts coarse aggregate; the rendering is one part cement to three of sand, and if the work is undertaken during hot weather the completed job must be kept damp for at least a fortnight by covering it with damp hessian or plastic sheeting. There are special preparations on the market for insulating the water from the concrete so that immediate planting or stocking with fish can take place, but two coats of a solution made from one part waterglass and four parts water is just as effective.

If butyl rubber sheeting is used the initial excavation must first be covered to a depth of 5 cm with fine sand to provide a smooth base. When the sheeting has been spread it must be temporarily weighed down with smooth stones, but once filled the weight of the water will mould it to the shape of the pond. The edges of the sheeting are best secured and concealed by means of flat stones laid around the margin, and although in this case it is not possible to grow true bog plants, primulas, astilbes, day lilies (*Hemerocallis*), hostas, iris, lythrum – all by nature marsh plants – will usually tolerate the somewhat drier conditions and can be relied upon to fit the bill. They will, of course, do as well or even better on the shelves of the concrete pond, and in this eminently satisfactory habitat a large patch of meadowsweet should certainly find a place, since it is one of the few marsh plants which produces seed that is attractive to birds.

In a small pond where only one or two lilies can be accommodated these are best planted in containers lowered into the water. The soil should be somewhat heavy and free from manure, and it must be rammed firmly into the container so that it does not loosen when wet. A top dressing of a couple of centimetres of clean shingle will ensure that it does not discolour the water. Some livestock – beetles and the larvae of various insects – will arrive uninvited, but a few water snails should be introduced as they help to keep the water clear by eating quantities of the algae.

The garden pond can be made to look quite a natural feature. It will be a focal point for most of the birds in the garden, whether for drinking or for bathing, and should therefore be visible from the house.

43

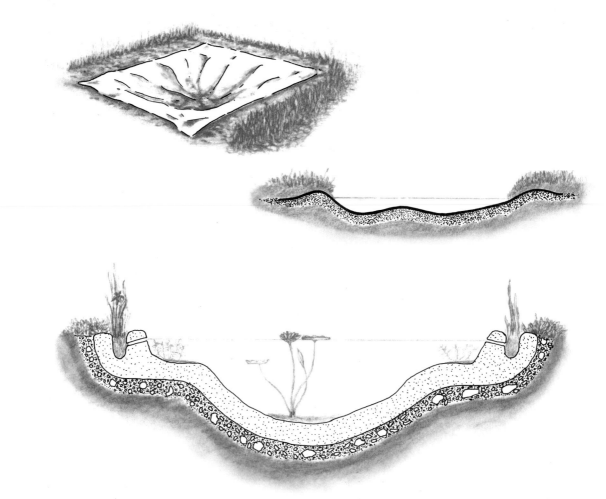

Above: A hole for a pond 30 cm deep, measuring 120 × 150 cm, has been dug. The polythene or butyl liner must measure 250 × 280 cm to allow for the depth of the pond and the overlap on the edges when filled with water, which pulls the liner down and moulds it to the shape of the pond. Centre: The pond is now filled with water and the edges of the liner have been covered with turf to give it a more natural look; a more hard-wearing edge can be made with paving stones. This little pond will become a great favourite with the birds but is too small for fish, which must have a depth of 50–60 cm to prevent them from freezing during the winter.

Below: This section through a concrete pond, 250 cm across and 60 cm deep, shows shelves round the edge for marginal aquatic plants, and a gutter, connected by inserted pipes to the main water surface, for bog-loving plants. It is quite big enough to hold a resident population of fish.

44

Fish can be a problem. If a junior member of the household can be persuaded to keep up a constant supply of minnows a Kingfisher might become a regular visitor to the garden. But if larger fish – goldfish for example – are provided the visitor could be a Grey Heron, and whereas a Kingfisher might be satisfied with one or two fish at a sitting the Grey Heron would probably clear the whole pond at a single visit. Just as Blue Tits learned about milk bottles, the Grey Heron has learned that these tiny patches of water contain food, and even urban gardens and those miles from the nearest heronry are no longer safe.

The one great disadvantage of a pond is that it will freeze at intervals during the winter, and there is little one can do about this. It is important, therefore, to arrange for a smaller water supply somewhere within sight of the bird table, and to get into the habit of topping it up every time the food is replenished. It is surprising how quickly half a dozen Starlings will empty a bird bath if they all get in together. An inverted tin dustbin lid is often suggested; concrete is probably better because the rough surface gives an improved foothold. The bath should be raised a little above ground level; a paving slab will provide a solid base for it, with three bricks arranged in the form of a triangle and the container on top. During frosty weather a wax nightlight placed in the cavity between the bricks should be sufficient to prevent the water freezing, and if a strong wind is blowing the gap between the bricks on the windward side can be closed to protect the candle. This is just one way of ensuring that water is constantly available.

46

3 Feeding devices

Although this chapter is entitled 'Feeding devices' it will be obvious from the preceding chapter that devices are hardly necessary. Birds will feed naturally from the ground or from trees and shrubs as they do in the wild, without the aid of any equipment. Man, of course, has devised for himself boxes of all shapes and sizes in which he may find warmth, shelter and utensils for eating and drinking, and the assumption seems to be that birds will appreciate these also. Some devices certainly provide protection for both nesting and feeding, but the main reason for their proliferation seems to be that they enable man to observe and enjoy the activities of the birds which are encouraged to come to his garden.

By providing food and water in the winter, man is making a contribution to the survival of small and vulnerable creatures, and in severe weather the effect of such help may be considerable. Whether it is a good thing or a bad thing for the laws of nature to be sidetracked in this way is a debatable matter. Harsh conditions ensure that only the fittest will survive, and supplementary feeding, by enabling some of the weaker members to do so, may ultimately have an adverse effect on the whole species. Man, however, is placing increasing strains on wildlife, and perhaps a little artificial help here and there may be forgiven. It is, in any case, difficult to ignore a hungry Robin standing in the snow.

Throwing out crumbs for the birds is probably one of man's oldest relationships with them, and is of course the simplest method of providing them with extra food; but just scattering food on the lawn or terrace can be very wasteful, and bird food other than kitchen

It is worth investing in a durable wire mesh hanging basket which prevents expensive food, such as peanuts, from being blown and scattered about. While Great Tits and Blue Tits enjoy extracting the nuts, other species like Dunnocks and Chaffinches will scavenge for fragments on the ground.

scraps is expensive to buy or time-consuming to collect from fields or hedgerows. On a lawn in particular some of the food is inevitably lost, and exotic plants may suddenly emerge in all sorts of odd places after a handful of 'wild bird seed' has been scattered.

Bird tables

In most gardens there will already be obvious places on which to put food, such as the top of a low wall, the slabs of a terrace or an old tree stump, but to most people feeding birds implies the provision of a bird table. Indeed a raised table has become so important that it is now almost standard garden furniture, although sometimes most unsuitably placed to serve the birds for which it is intended.

There are so many different designs of bird table on the market that it may be difficult to decide which to choose. Some are fairly expensive, and there is no reason why they should not be made at home. All that is really needed is a flat piece of wood fixed to the top of an upright of some sort. Of course food placed on this platform would soon be blown off by the wind or scattered by the birds' activities, so a rim about 2.5 cm high placed round the edge, with a

Feeding at ground level

One of the best ways of presenting food on the ground is to place it on a large piece of wood, preferably with a rim round the edges to prevent the food from falling off, and if this is to be placed on a lawn, raised about 5 cm (2 inches) so that the grass underneath can 'breathe'. Better still is a longer and narrower piece of wood such as a plank or an old door. The food may be spread thinly along the length of it, and this tends to separate the birds linear fashion which eliminates much squabbling. This method can be used on a terrace too, and the less aggressive species get a chance to join in. After a fall of snow it is almost essential to use a board of some sort, unless it is possible to keep an area clear, since food thrown on to soft snow quickly disappears from sight. A further advantage of a board is that it can be taken in at night so that rats are not encouraged. Some birds such as Dunnocks, thrushes, Blackbirds and Chaffinches prefer to eat from the ground, so some food should always be provided in this way.

Above: Members of the crow family, especially Rooks, may monopolise a bird table, and the large sprig of gorse here has not deterred this Rook. It is better to construct an overhanging roof to the table, divide foods such as lumps of bread, meat and bones into smaller portions, and spread them over a wide area so that large pieces cannot be snatched and carried away.

gap at each corner for drainage, is an improvement. The upright is not essential, as the tray can be hung from the branch of a tree or from a clothes line, or suspended from a bracket screwed to a wall or fence post. A roof is not vital, although most commercial tables have one, and it certainly gives some protection to both birds and food during heavy rain or a snow storm. It may also deter a Sparrowhawk from swooping at small birds feeding, since the space over the table will be restricted, but these are minor advantages. The RSPB have an excellent leaflet written by John Thornton and illustrated by Robert Gillmor called *D.I.Y. Bird Table.*

Of the commercial tables, the RSPB market a well-made model with a roof which can be supplied either ready for fixing to a 5 cm square upright post, as a hanging table complete with chains and ring, or with a bracket for fixing to a wall or fence. As an extra refinement a seed hopper can be fitted under the roof. A similar design but without the hopper is the traditional bird table manufactured by Jamie Wood Ltd. This also has a roof and is supplied with a 1.5 metre pole for inserting into the ground. It has two hooks beneath the table on which food containers, bones or nut bags may be hung. Both these tables are strongly constructed and there is very little difference in the price. Either would look well in any garden. A smaller version of the table top is made by Jamie Wood Ltd, which they call a feeding tray; it is specifically for hanging from a bough or line.

The bird table does not necessarily have to be rectangular. The Rikden Small Bird Feeder has been designed so that a number of birds can feed at the same time. It is made of resin-impregnated fibreglass and the food is contained in a narrow circular trough 30 cm in diameter round the edge of the table. The idea is that birds perch on the rim of the trough so that the food is not fouled by droppings. It has a cone-shaped roof larger than the table, which is low enough to prevent large birds from alighting on the feeding surface. This too is designed to hang from a branch or from a wire stretched between two points, or again a bracket can be supplied for suspending the table from a post or window frame.

Pippaware make a circular table, which is in effect a plastic tray 34 cm in diameter, with a central recess for holding drinking water and drainage holes around the edge. These holes may be used for suspending strings of peanuts, lumps of fat or bones. It is supplied with a 1.4 metre steel pole in four sections, the end one fitted with a spike for insertion into the ground or lawn. The advantage of this type of table is that it is very light, easy to move and to clean, but stability may be a problem, especially in a high wind.

The most sophisticated of commercial designs is the Sussex Bird Table made by Jamie Wood Ltd. This is a two-tier feeding device, the upper part of which is designed for small birds only. This part is enclosed between the gable roof and the floor by strong $1\frac{1}{2} \times 1$ inch (38×25 mm) green plastic-covered wire mesh, which gives it the appearance of a rectangular bird cage. It is completely squirrel proof, and inside is suspended a cylindrical $\frac{1}{4}$ inch (6.3 mm) wire mesh nut container, held horizontally by metal handles on hooks from the roof. This holds about 1 kilogram of peanuts, and access for filling and cleaning is by way of a portcullis-type wire door which is spring loaded. The lower feeding tier consists of a green plastic tray, suspended 16.5 cm from the corners of the top half by hooks. This is very easy to clean, can be used for any scraps of food, and enables larger birds to feed here. The upper table and roof are made of waterproof exterior-bonded plywood, so no preservative should be required, but the manufacturers recommend a thin dressing of linseed oil, which is harmless to birds. This enhances the appearance of the wooden parts, which develop a golden colour contrasting pleasantly with the dark green of pole and tray and blending with the natural colours of the garden.

At first sight the Sussex Bird Table may appear to be rather complicated, and there were some doubts as to whether birds would use it if other more easily accessible food was available nearby. In one instance, however, it took Blue Tits only twenty minutes to discover the way in to the peanuts. The manufacturers give the roof

Five tried and tested commercial and home-made bird tables and trays: above left, RSPB Bird Table suspended with seed hopper in place; below left, Jamie Wood Ltd Sussex Bird Table; centre, Tratten Bird Feeder; above right, simple hanging feeding tray; below right, double seed hopper with central divider enabling food to be dispensed both sides of the table.

measurements as 17×10 inches (43×25 cm) and 12 inches (30 cm) high, but this gives an exaggerated impression of the size of the actual feeding area, which is only 30×19 cm. With a large peanut holder suspended in this space there is little room left for the birds: it is noticeable that even Blue Tits appear to crouch beneath the nut holder, and if they hang under it with fully extended legs, their backs touch the table. Shortening the handles by which the peanut holder is suspended raises it a little, but even then the birds' tails sweep the floor. The only solution seems to be to unhook the container and stand it vertically, or to substitute a smaller one which would need to be filled more frequently.

This table is strong and weatherproof and is very successful in keeping off unwanted predators; perhaps a slightly larger version of the existing model would enable small birds to feed with the same security but greater comfort. Normally it is supplied with a 1.5 metre pole for inserting into the ground or with a patio base as an extra. It is of course possible to surround a home-made model with wire netting to exclude Starlings and squirrels, but it would be difficult to make either that or a conventional one treated in the same way as aesthetically attractive as the Sussex table.

There are innumerable designs of non-proprietary 'rustic' type bird tables which can be purchased at most garden centres, but you should examine these carefully before buying. Many of them are made of birch wood, and while the silver bark is attractive initially, it soon peels off and the wood has a very short life when exposed to the elements. Some have elegantly or grotesquely twisted branches used as supporting poles, often with smaller feeding platforms placed at lower levels than the main table. These platforms make ideal resting places for cats and the rough wood offers excellent claw sharpening facilities before the final pounce! Squirrels too can climb these with the minimum of effort and will soon polish off any food on the top table. It is difficult to deter hungry squirrels, but this is surely making life too easy for them.

Straw-thatched roofs may be pretty to look at but they have little else to recommend them. The straw quickly disintegrates, and will be enthusiastically carried away by nest-building Starlings and House Sparrows. Some of these tables are made with a nesting box in the gable roof, with an entrance hole so small that even a Blue Tit would have difficulty in squeezing in. However, having criticised this, it is known that a family of Pied Flycatchers was successfully reared in just such a box in a garden in Cumbria.

Not all birds feed by the same method: some prefer to take food from the ground or from a wide flat surface, some are acrobatic feeders and others are able to cling on and probe into cracks and crevices. It would seem obvious therefore that the greater the number and variety of feeding devices provided in the garden the greater will be the number and diversity of species one might expect to attract.

Replenishing your feeders

Artificial food is fairly expensive to buy, so some attention should be given to the type and quantity of food which can reasonably be supplied with regularity throughout the winter, for once feeding has started the local bird population will come to rely on it being maintained. The sudden falling off of supplies during a hard spell of weather may do untold harm, for the birds will not be able to find natural foods to compensate for the loss. Far better to provide a reasonable amount each day and to supplement this in times of real hardship. In any case, few people could provide food on the scale of one enthusiastic observer, who regretted that due to the huge increase in the price of peanuts he had reluctantly been compelled to reduce his winter's supply from six to five hundredweight!

Many newcomers to garden bird feeding, having exhausted their kitchen scraps, will provide the red nylon mesh bags filled with peanuts which are sold in most pet shops. These contain only a small quantity of nuts and are a most expensive way of buying them. Birds consume nuts voraciously, especially in cold weather, and besides the parties of tits which frequent them, large numbers of Greenfinches, Starlings, House Sparrows and even Jays become adept at hanging on. The bags will soon be torn to pieces and the contents spilled on the ground, where the less aggressive species will find it difficult to compete. However it is worth providing nuts in this manner if there are Siskins in the locality, because these delightful birds do seem to be attracted by the brightly coloured bags. Perhaps this was the reason for the rather astonishing sight seen in Ireland in 1979. In a small front garden on a main road grew a small fruit tree, and strung along its branches like lanterns on a Christmas tree were some thirty or so red nut bags – but not a bird in sight!

Put out food at three levels to cater for varied feeding habits and tastes. The Nuthatch (left) is happiest clinging to a nut-filled hanging basket, the delicate Long-tailed Tit (top) prefers the safety of a flat raised surface, while the Dunnock (below) will be content to pick and probe at fragments on the ground.

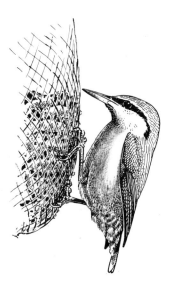

The most economical way of buying nuts, whether split or whole, is to obtain them in bulk from a pet shop or from a reputable wholesaler. The expense may seem great initially, but a large delivery lasts a long time and can be shared between neighbours and friends.

Hanging feeding devices

There are many hanging devices for food on the market, and catalogues of these may be obtained from the manufacturers. Containers of various designs are usually on sale in garden centres and pet shops, and it is advisable to compare prices and suitability of purpose before buying. Any pattern of $\frac{1}{4}$ inch (6.3 mm) wire mesh container will prove satisfactory for nuts, kitchen scraps and pieces of fat or suet; if the wire is plastic coated, so much the better. Galvanised wire will serve equally well, and if given a coat of black paint before being brought into service will last that much longer. The RSPB market a very good small food cage, 5×3 inches (12.7×7.6 cm), made of plastic-coated wire mesh; it is fitted with a lid and has a metal handle at the top. These are reasonably priced, withstand being attacked by dogs and chewed by squirrels and will last for years. A similar type can be obtained from the Scottish National Institute for the War Blinded, who also make a galvanised nut cylinder with a smaller mesh.

Jamie Wood Ltd. have a hanging container called a Tit-haven which is supplied as a do-it-yourself kit complete with all accessories and instructions. It is a little like a mini bird table, with bars round it and a feeder tray inside which is removable for cleaning. They also produce a really excellent nut container called the 'Giant size squirrel and starling proof tit feeder' which really appears to live up to its name. It is a vertical cylinder holding about half a kilogram of nuts in an inner $\frac{1}{4}$ inch (6.3 mm) wire mesh container, the whole being protected by 2.5 mm green plastic-coated wire. The actual container is 28 cm deep by 9 cm in diameter, with stout handles at either end, and a strong base and lid, making the overall height 46 cm. This needs to be filled far less frequently than other devices and appears to work satisfactorily.

Three more RSPB models must be mentioned. If it is considered desirable to confine the feeding of peanuts to species which are able to feed upside down, then there is a wooden box with a sliding base for use when filling, and a wire mesh end. This is hung with the mesh underneath so that only the most agile species can get at the food. The other two feeders are both made of transparent acrylic, so that birds and food supply are easily seen. The Dinabird Feeder is a covered tube 40 cm high with a handle for suspending it. At various

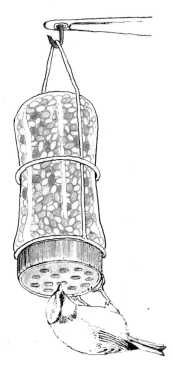

Below: Inverted hanging jars can be used to allow the acrobatic tits to feed on peanuts which less agile birds, such as House Sparrows and Starlings, cannot reach. Any sort of screw-top jar with holes drilled in the lid can be used, but large Kilner jars equipped with aluminium sheet inserts drilled with holes contain plenty of nuts and are very satisfactory.

Above: The plastic net bags in which we buy certain vegetables, fruit and nuts make good hanging containers – but only temporary ones – for larger food scraps such as fat, suet and bird cake. Great Tits and Blue Tits can destroy this mesh, which soon becomes messy and needs replacing.

points along the tube there are perches, and above each perch a porthole from which the birds can feed. It can be used for a mixture of foods, such as crushed oats and seed, or for nuts, and the food is kept dry. The other feeder, which has a plastic ring on the top for hanging, is a clear globe which is filled through a small hole at the top with a press-down lid. The food drops through a funnel into the bottom half of the globe and the birds are supposed to reach it through three holes. There is a down-sloping rim running round the centre. If this feeder is filled with minced peanuts, tits will quickly learn to feed at the holes, and this type of food will drop through the funnel fairly successfully if shaken down from time to time. Farinaceous food, however, tends to stick in the funnel when damp, and as this does not appear to be popular, few birds will make an attempt to feed. In a strong wind the globe is blown sideways, and food spills from the holes. One observer reported that the hanging ring broke very quickly and the filling lid came off. However, another globe has been used successfully for a whole winter filled only with minced peanuts, and although other species have been seen to hover close to it, only the tits have succeeded in taking food.

Home-made bird cake in the form of a hanging ball, based on rendered down fat, gives you an opportunity to get rid of kitchen scraps of bread, cake, nuts, cheese and so on, and is appreciated by other species as well as Blue Tits.

One drawback is that Blue Tits will actually go through the holes into the globe where they may foul the rest of the food.

All gravity feed containers have two disadvantages. If the food gets damp it will clog, and the feeder may need to be dismantled in order to get it running freely again, and if a seed mixture is used, birds will scatter it in order to find their preferred items. Much of the seed may then be wasted. The solution is to fill the hopper with one type of seed only – for example wheat, oats or millet.

Since there are now so many different and satisfactory designs of nut feeders available, there is one which might well be discontinued.

This is the spiral feeder, a cylindrical coil of plastic-covered wire like a spring, into which the nuts are placed so that birds can feed from between the coils. With the continual comings and goings the coils tend to expand and contract and sometimes the birds' claws may be trapped (once, in the case of a Coal Tit, the tongue was caught). Spiral feeders can be bought at most pet shops, and the RSPB produce one which may be hung on a bird table or tree, and it can now also be obtained with a special adapter and suction pad for suspending it on the outside of a window. Unless this type of feeder can be made completely safe it would be better to invest in a different design, and the RSPB do have another window feeder which is virtually a tray to fix to the sill. It has two shallow bowls, one for food and the other for water.

Another useful device for presenting a different kind of food is the tit bell. This can in fact be any cup-shaped object filled with a mixture of fruit, seeds and brown bread, set into melted fat. It is then hung upside down on a branch or the corner of the bird table where it will attract a number of acrobatic birds. A half coconut shell will do, and there are a whole range of hollowed-out hardwood bells available including an attractive one from the Scottish National Institute for the War Blinded. At the top end of the price scale is the Tony Soper ceramic bell on sale in some gift shops, but the wooden ones are functional and will not break so easily.

A Long-tailed Tit feeding at a do-it-yourself scrap basket – in this case an old chip basket from inside a deep fryer. These tiny birds, increasingly frequent visitors to bird tables all over Britain, are particularly fond of fat and suet.

Home-made food dispensers

Many variations on these devices can be made at home very simply and cheaply. For a seed hopper, an inverted bottle full of seed, suspended a few millimetres above a small tray, will allow a little to escape initially and more to be released as this is eaten. If the seed comes out too quickly the bottle needs to be lowered until the correct flow is achieved.

A short length of bough from an old tree can be drilled with 2.5 cm holes. These can then be filled with dripping or bird pudding. With a screw-eye in one end the bough can be hung in a tree, where it makes an excellent feeder for tits, Nuthatches or even Great Spotted Woodpeckers. An old tree stump or a log standing on end can be treated in the same fashion, making an attractive and natural looking feature in the garden and fulfilling a useful purpose also; this could provide a dignified end for a dead elm tree.

A cheap and effective way of dispensing peanuts to the local titmice is to make use of an inverted glass jar suspended by a bracket from a wall or post (see diagram). A Kilner jar is ideal, in which case the glass top needs to be replaced by a circular perforated disc made of aluminium, formica or even plastic floor tiles. The size of the holes drilled in the plate is dictated by the size of the peanuts used: 6 mm holes for small round peanuts and 8 mm holes for larger ones. The holes should be drilled close together and the surface filed smooth to avoid the risks posed by jagged edges. An ordinary screw-top jar may also be used on the same principle. The cage needed to support the inverted jar may be made of rot-proof cord or of wire, and the jar can easily be taken down to replenish the nut supply. It may take a little while for the tits to fathom the access route to the visible peanuts but once discovered the habit spreads rapidly. Very few House Sparrows or Greenfinches are ever capable of clinging successfully to the jar but they may stab at the nuts while hovering alongside before exiting to allow the more agile titmice to gain access to the food.

Water containers

Whilst giving every attention to the feeding of birds, do not forget that water for drinking and bathing is just as necessary. Every well equipped bird garden provides water, and to stand by a window in summer and watch a family of Spotted Flycatchers taking turns to bathe in an up-turned dustbin lid (p. 45 and opposite) is a delight which is not to be missed.

Almost any saucer-shaped vessel is suitable if it is fairly small and shallow and has a reasonably rough surface; even a plastic dog bowl can be a favourite place for small birds to bathe. However, there is a large selection of commercially made models. The RSPB market a bird drinking tray 12 × 17 inches (30 × 43 cm) in natural-coloured fibreglass which is quite attractive and very easy to clean. Jamie Wood Ltd. make a 14 × 10 inch (36 × 25 cm) shallow tray on a pole. There is also the Rikden Bird Bath, a 20 inch (50 cm) circular bowl made of resin-impregnated fibreglass. Each one is individually made, and stands on three short, well-rounded legs to keep it clear of the ground or lawn and prevent it from tilting. It is a soft olive green on the outside and natural sand colour inside, while the floor which slopes very gently has a sanded surface to give good claw hold. The bird bath is very light and easy to clean and the makers claim that even if the water in it freezes solid, it can be thawed with a kettle full of boiling water and no harm will be done.

Garden centres usually have a bewildering choice of bird baths and drinking vessels of every shape and size, sculptured in almost anything from nice stone to nasty plastic. Birds won't mind whether they drink from a shell held by a naiad or from the navel of a fat little Buddha – the choice is ours, not theirs.

It should of course be remembered that with any water container freezing will be a problem at some time each winter. A hollow rubber ball placed in the water will help to take the strain of the ice in a breakable bowl, but on no account should any kind of anti-freeze, glycerine or salt be used. These can cause untold damage to the birds' feather structure or prove toxic.

By setting an up-turned dustbin lid into the ground or grass you can improvise an ideal small bird bath, at which elusive species like Hawfinches may appear. Cracking large, hard fruits such as cherry, hornbeam, beech and sycamore is thirsty work and they may travel long distances for water. Unable to suck it up, the Hawfinch repeatedly fills its bill and mouth with water and raises its head, letting the water run down its throat.

Positioning of feeding devices

The siting of the bird table, of the various feeding and drinking devices, and even the selection of the area where ground feeding is to take place need a considerable amount of thought. The safety of the birds should always be the primary consideration. Any feeding area should be away from thick cover where a lurking cat might hide; on the other hand a bird table isolated in the middle of a large lawn would attract very few birds. If feeding habits are watched closely it soon becomes apparent that birds like a perching place, a tree perhaps, some two or three metres away from the feeding area or table from which they can take stock of the situation before making a direct assault on the food. If there are many birds present this often becomes a queuing place for those awaiting their turn. In the event of a surprise attack from a predator, or even the movement of people at a window, birds will 'scramble' to this safe area, so a certain amount of cover not too far away is essential. This applies even more forcibly when birds are bathing, for they become very absorbed in this activity and are less likely to notice a predator, and wet feathers may prove a hindrance in making a quick getaway. A

During the autumn and winter, Long-tailed Tits move around our woods and hedges in flocks, accompanied by other small birds including Blue Tits. Once they discover an open-topped bird table suitably stocked with grated cheese and breadcrumbs they may well patronise that garden regularly.

compromise is therefore desirable: not too close to cover where danger may lurk, not too far away from necessary safety. It must not be forgotten that it is an advantage to be able to watch all that is going on from a window, and a house makes a very cosy hide in the middle of winter!

Ensuring that the devices are safe and clean

As winter is the time of year when artificial feeding is mostly undertaken, all devices for feeding, drinking and bathing will have to stand up to the worst of the weather. If the bird table is on a pole, this must be strong enough to take the strain of a howling gale and set firmly enough into the ground to prevent rocking. If on a base, it must be large and heavy enough to prevent it from blowing over.

It is a good idea at the beginning of the winter to ensure that all equipment is in good order. The life of it may well be prolonged by the replacing of missing nails or screws, and galvanised ones are worth the little extra cost for all outside carpentry. A dressing of copper-based preservative will help to prolong the life of wooden items. Ragged pieces of wire netting and the remains of thread from hanging peanuts could be real hazards to birds. It is far more pleasant to do these jobs while the mellow autumn sun still shines than to leave them until frost has gripped the garden.

It cannot be emphasised too often that cleanliness is important. All feeding devices and receptacles should be scrubbed from time to time, and it is a good plan to move the bird table occasionally and alter the position of the hanging devices. This allows the ground beneath to sweeten and the grass to recover from the attentions of a density of birds.

Although only a small selection of feeding and drinking utensils has been described in this chapter, it will give you some idea of what is available and what you can make yourself. Personal choice is important and improvisation and experiment are part of the fun. There is also a great deal of satisfaction to be gained from giving feeding devices as presents, in the knowledge that yet another garden may be giving extra help to birds in winter, as well as added pleasure and interest to friends.

4 Types of food to provide

Many people claim, when asked, that they feed the birds during winter, but in most cases a closer investigation reveals that 'feeding the birds' merely consists of throwing out stale bread and other oddments of household waste as and when they become available. Modern bird feeding methods have progressed much further than this, and it is interesting to ponder how far the commercial exploitation of wild bird feeding has influenced the trend.

Without doubt it is very much easier to shake a packet of prepared bird food on to the bird table than it is to prepare a home-made bird cake, and if the plastic bag of peanuts has only to be hooked on to the nearest nail or twig this is much easier than having to take down the container, fill it, store away the remainder of the loose nuts and re-hang the container, all perhaps with the temperature well below zero. This approach has the disadvantage of being expensive, but it certainly seems to be popular with a wide cross-section of the general public.

The advantages of ready-made bird food are obvious; they appeal to the elderly who, on a cold morning, want to get indoors again as quickly as possible; they appeal to the busy mums who have to get the family off to school – in short they appeal to a very large part of the community who, while they would not claim to be ornithologists or even avid birdwatchers, like to see birds around the house and are prepared to go to a little trouble to attract them. If we can persuade these people to extend their activities a little, this book will have been worthwhile.

Coconut flesh is popular with tits, especially the Blue Tit. Saw the nut in half and suspend each by a wire or cord so that the rain cannot get in. Always serve coconut in the shell, never desiccated or ground, as this swells up inside the bird's stomach with disastrous results. Empty shells can be used as fat receptacles.

Regularity is very important. Ideally food should be available at all times, but if the volume of food required to achieve this becomes excessive – and word soon gets around in the bird community – then the rations should appear at the same time each day. Birds very quickly learn to fall in with the householder's programme, and if the food appears at 9 a.m. every day they will be ready and waiting for it; they will learn equally quickly that when it has gone they must move on to a neighbouring garden or into the woods to search for beechmast or berries. The danger is that having become accustomed to this pattern they arrive one cold morning to find nothing there. In this case they will hang around hopefully, wasting the short daylight hours when they should be building up reserves to last them through the long night.

The range of foods to offer

Variety is the next requirement. The wider the range of food offered, the greater the number of species one can hope to attract. Readily available foods come under six main headings: nuts, meat, fats, fruit, seeds and grain-based foods.

Nuts

The nuts most commonly used are peanuts which, since this is a tropical crop, have to be purchased. Brazil nuts, hazel nuts and walnuts are all readily taken if the shells are opened sufficiently to enable the birds to get at the kernel; half a walnut will keep the tits happy for a whole day since they can only extract the kernel with

Foiling the grey squirrel

Grey squirrels are the bane of the bird feeder's life; they will go to almost any length to obtain peanuts and are quite capable of stealing not only the nuts but the container as well. Various deterrents are worth trying. An inverted metal cone fitted to the pole of the bird table in the manner of the anti-rat devices used on ships' hawsers in British ports will prevent them climbing up, but if there is anything nearby which can be climbed they will scale it and they can jump quite impressive distances. A container designed specifically to foil squirrels has been marketed by Jamie Wood Ltd in Sussex (see p. 50) and this is the most successful attempt yet at solving the problem.

Birds often develop individual food tastes. This particular Jay in a Scottish garden was attracted by peanuts, but also became fond of porridge and toasted bread, protesting strongly if the food was not to its liking.

difficulty. There are various grades of peanut. High-grade nuts fit for human consumption are expensive; the smaller nuts usually sold as bird food are good, but no better than the broken nuts which have lost their outer skins, which often cost considerably less and can be purchased more cheaply still in bulk. Peanuts in the shell are not very economical but their entertainment value is high; the amount of energy a Nuthatch will put into hacking one open has to be seen to be believed. The kernels are usually provided in plastic-covered wire containers which can be refilled or in soft orange-coloured plastic bags (but note the reservations about these on p. 53).

Whatever the container, peanuts will attract a wide spectrum of species. All the tits, including locally the Long-tailed, Greenfinches, House Sparrows, Nuthatches, Siskins and even woodpeckers have mastered the art of clinging to the containers and extracting the nuts; Chaffinches try hard but usually with relatively little success and Dunnocks tend to be content to pick up the fragments which fall to the ground below. Some Robins employ a different technique: they hover beside the nuts and make quick jabs with their bills without attempting to cling to the container.

65

Meat

Cooked meat, on or off the bone, may be offered, but raw meat should be resisted as it may carry harmful organisms that can induce food poisoning. Meat again is attractive to a number of other forms of animal life besides birds. Cats are the worst, since their presence threatens the birds themselves as well as the food. Water, hurled in large quantities from a bedroom window, is effective, but a cat-proof fence is better. A stray dog will carry away a week's meat or suet ration at one visit, but at least dogs cannot climb and attention to the fences and gates should solve this. Nocturnal visits by foxes are probably far more common even in urban areas than most people realise and foxes, too, are meat eaters. As far as possible, therefore, any type of meat or bone should be hung as high as possible: 2.5–3 metres is not too much if it can be achieved, and if the butcher has been kind and the offering is particularly large it might even be worthwhile taking it in at night.

Many species will appreciate bones. Woodpeckers, crows, Coal Tits and Nuthatches will be regular visitors, but almost anything may turn up. A most unusual visitor to a Surrey garden during the

Many birds, including crows, gulls, woodpeckers and Starlings, delight in picking the remains of meat from bones and carcases. Here a Jackdaw is deftly using its foot to extract the much-loved marrow. Never put out raw meat or bones that have been in contact with uncooked food of animal origin.

exceptionally severe winter of 1962/63 was a Tawny Owl, perched on a large meat bone in broad daylight. Marrow bones are also useful and can often be bought cheaply from the butcher; they should be sawn in half to expose the marrow and are best presented in open scrap baskets, attracting a range of birds from Rook to Goldcrest.

Fats

Fat comes in many forms; all are useful and none should be wasted. At the top of the list is suet, of which good large lumps should be pierced with a wooden skewer and hung out of the reach of hungry quadrupeds. Some species, particularly Siskins, seem to like their suet a little 'high' so the remains of the offering should not be disposed of too quickly.

Mutton fat is good when rendered down because it sets rock-hard and is the ideal base for a bird cake, but all sorts of fat scraps can be pressed into service for this and the birds do not seem to mind if the various kinds are mixed. Butchers' trimmings, the scraps cut away from the Sunday joint, even the contents of the pan in which the chicken was roasted are suitable. All should be put into a pan kept specially for the purpose and heated slowly with the kitchen windows and door wide open. When the liquid is bubbling gently and the solids are a nice golden brown, the brew is ready. The solids should be removed and, when cool, put into the scrap basket; the liquid has a variety of uses.

A little liquid fat poured on to the rough bark of a tree may be discovered by one or other of the less pugnacious species which are often scarce visitors to the bird table. (It is best placed on the north-facing side, since even winter sun will melt fat.) Long-tailed Tits, having made the discovery, will become regular and punctual visitors, always arriving early in the morning and again on their way to roost, with a couple of well-spaced visits in between. As a special treat a little grated cheese may be placed near their feeding area just before their expected time of arrival. Long-tails love cheese, but so do most other garden feeding birds, so if it is put out with the normal rations there is rarely any left when they arrive. Other visitors to the fat-coated branches or tree trunk, although never in such large numbers, are Goldcrests, Wrens, Treecreepers and maybe even the delightful but rare little Firecrest.

Many of the commoner visitors to the bird table are the rather aggressive species – tits, Starlings, Greenfinches and House Sparrows – so it is advisable to have secondary feeding arrangements scattered as widely around the garden as possible, and other forms of fat-dispenser are ideal for this. Pine cones, the larger the better, can be coated with hot fat, allowed to cool and hung around the garden like

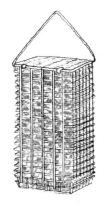

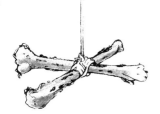

Above: A lidded fat and oddments container made from square 2.5 cm or 2.5 × 1.2 cm weld mesh. The grid should not be too large as smaller pieces of fat etc. will fall through. Left-over bones can be tied together with wire or string, and hung from a bird table or tree bough.

The Great Spotted Woodpecker is wary, but feeds increasingly in rural gardens. It will habitually wedge a nut into a tree crevice to deal with it, and can be encouraged if you drill holes and fill them with peanuts or larger nuts: here a male has come for hazelnuts.

Christmas tree decorations. Tit bells (see p. 57) are hollowed-out blocks of wood into which the fat can be poured, but equally satisfactory are the empty half-shells of coconuts, and these also make excellent moulds for a bird cake.

The ingredients for a bird cake can be almost anything which is normally offered in other ways. Its great advantage is that the birds cannot carry it away and hide it as they will do with loose peanuts, sunflower seeds, etc. Coal Tits and Marsh Tits are the worst in this respect; they will fly back and forth incessantly until every loose nut or seed has been carried away and hidden. Fat is not normally offered on the ground, but during very cold weather fat and cheese crumbs may be scattered amongst the leaf litter beneath the bushes where they may be found by Wrens. This will provide them with a valuable food source during a difficult period.

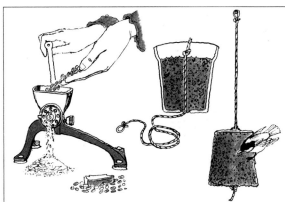

Making a bird cake

The larger ingredients such as meat, peanuts and cheese-rind should be finely chopped or, preferably, passed through a mincing machine; stale cake and broken biscuits should be crumbled, and if the mixture is still rather damp a good measure of oatmeal can be added. Mix it all up thoroughly, then pour the hot fat over it and put it into moulds to set. Cake making takes a little time but is well worth the effort, for in this way all the birds get a fair share of everything and nothing is carried away and wasted.

Fruit

When the weather is mild during the autumn and early winter the thrushes should find life fairly easy. Worms which remained deep in the ground during the hot summer days are active now in the dew-laden grass, and the hedgerows are heavy with a succession of berry-bearing crops; and even if the first frosts arrive early to lock up the subterranean larder, the remnants of the wild fruit crop are usually sufficient to tide the birds over for a week or so. After Christmas the position can deteriorate rapidly. The wild fruit supply will become exhausted, and the fallen berries will have been carried away to their winter stores by a host of small mammals. If the weather remains mild all is well, for there is still plenty of food just below the surface of the turf, but with a succession of frosts the situation can be critical. Readily obtainable food will vanish overnight after a really hard frost, and until the thaw comes the thrushes must eke out a precarious existence turning over fallen leaves beneath the hedges and in woodland in the hope of finding a few dormant grubs. It is now that they need our assistance.

Of course, the resident Blackbirds and Song Thrushes will have been around the garden throughout the autumn and they will have supplemented their natural foods from the bird table whenever they chose to do so, but the winter thrushes, the Redwings and Fieldfares, are not often driven into many gardens before Christmas, and even the Mistle Thrush is a rather unusual visitor until after the turn of the year. So if the quantity of fruit set aside for the birds during the winter is limited it is wise to hold most of it back, or at least to ration it, until the really severe weather arrives.

Fruit for the birds usually means apples, occasionally pears. They will eat a number of other fruits – figs, grapes, currants and raisins, dried apricots and prunes, but these are usually only available if the cook decrees that they have been in her store-cupboard too long. If this happens any of the dried fruit should be soaked in water over-night before being offered to the birds.

Apples and pears should be scattered around on the ground over as wide an area as possible. If they are confined to a small area around the bird table a particularly territory-minded Mistle Thrush is likely to spend most of his day driving off any other bird which ventures into his domain. It helps if the outer skin of the apple is broken; the birds rarely start on a new apple until the whole of the contents of an opened fruit have been consumed. And if you see a Marsh Tit eyeing the proceedings with interest, don't be surprised. He does not want the fruit – he is waiting for the pips! The fruit does not have to be first-grade Cox's Orange Pippins of course. Any apples, no matter how bruised and battered, will do – even the sourest little green crab apples will be tackled if conditions are really hard.

Birds do not care for citrus fruits but Nuthatches, woodpeckers and the tits are fond of another tropical fruit, the coconut. Few other species will touch it, probably because they are not equipped to chip off small fragments of the hard kernel. Sawn in half and hung a little way from the bird table they will help ease the congestion around the table, and the empty shells are useful as food receptacles.

Surplus autumn apples and pears are best stored and put out in the winter when conditions are severe. Here a Redwing is feeding on apples in the snow.

In addition to orchard fruit there is a wide range of fruit and berries which may be harvested and stored in season. Berries of the rowan, hawthorn and holly from the hedgerow, and cotoneaster, berberis and cherry laurel from the garden are among the most useful. They can be air dried, stored in a cool place safe from the attentions of wood mice, and offered in small quantities on the bird table from time to time. Alternatively, depending upon what control the bird feeder has over the domestic arrangements, they can be deep frozen – a method which preserves the natural juices and makes them more attractive to the birds.

Seeds

It is probably no accident that it is generally the commoner British finches which frequent the garden feeding sites. These are the species which have adapted to the changing conditions around them, and their ability and willingness to accept unfamiliar foods may play an important part in achieving for them a slightly higher survival rate. Greenfinches and to a lesser extent Chaffinches will eat almost any seed that the pet shop or corn merchant can supply, from the large hard grains of cereals to the smallest of weed seeds. Since feeding birds on a large scale can be expensive, it is sensible to choose one of the cheaper seeds as the bulk item and keep a little of the more expensive seed for the more fastidious feeders as and when they arrive. Siskins, for example, are passionately fond of an imported seed called niger, but the Greenfinches and Chaffinches can get on very well without it.

A number of firms make up a 'wild bird' mixture especially for garden bird feeding. Some of these are exceedingly good; others unfortunately appear to have been diluted with a large amount of waste and otherwise unsaleable rubbish. The best plan is to try a little from several sources, and then to examine the tray of the bird table carefully when the birds have had an opportunity to feed from it. If a consistently high proportion of certain seeds are not being consumed the mixture is not a good one and a change is indicated.

Some of the ingredients in these 'wild bird' mixtures can be bought separately. Canary seed is an imported grass which will occasionally ripen its seed in Britain. Rape seed and charlock are members of the cabbage family which were once sown extensively by farmers who ploughed in the resulting vegetation as green manure. Hemp is another small seed attractive to all the finches, to Skylark and Meadow Pipit, and to the tits which, because they cannot crack open the rather large seed in any other way, hold it beneath their claws and hammer away with tremendous energy and unerring accuracy – which is just as well since they look as if they

71

are likely to cripple themselves for life at any moment! Sunflower seed is an oily seed, valuable during cold weather, but unfortunately the tits will carry most of it away and hide it, thus defeating one of the objects of attracting birds into the garden.

Seed can be dispensed from a hopper, spread on the bird table, scattered on short grass or bare earth, or presented in all such ways. Bramblings and Siskins seem to like to have their seed in grass while Redpolls and Meadow Pipits prefer the bare ground, and providing that the amount supplied is carefully controlled there should be no problem of seed germinating later on. The birds will see to that.

In addition to the commercial seeds there are a number, both wild and cultivated, which can be collected and stored for winter use. They should be harvested when ripe, the stems being cut a few inches below the seed heads and tied in bunches. These bunches should be wrapped in muslin or placed in large paper bags; it is essential to allow the air to circulate around them so polythene bags should be avoided. A complete list of the plants which might be treated in this way would run to many pages and would include most of our common native weeds. Unfortunately a great deal of effort, and storage space, is required to produce a rather insignificant amount of seed, so harvesting activities are best limited to a few plants which can be relied upon to give a reasonable return. Sunflower heads, teasel, honesty, cabbage, knapweed, thistle, dock, ragwort and hemp agrimony are among the best.

The seed heads of five plants well worth collecting in autumn so that you can put them out in the garden feeding area in winter. Left to right, top to bottom: honesty, wild cabbage, ragwort, dock and hemp agrimony.

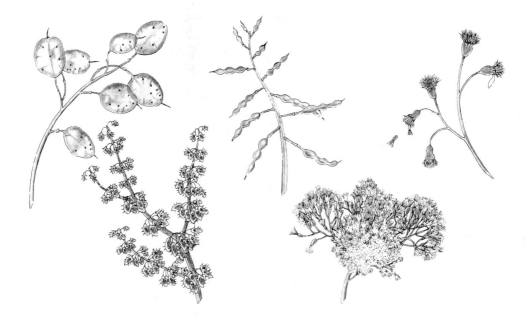

Above: When natural seed supplies, especially beech mast, are exhausted Bramblings often enter gardens in large numbers to feed on a variety of small seeds. In cold weather they may be accompanied by birds such as the Tree Sparrow (centre right).

Grain-based foods

Bread, biscuits and stale cake are the farinaceous foods most likely to be available from the kitchen as bird food. At one time bread was the main food offered to birds, and a controversy arose as to whether white or brown bread was better. (Not that it had much effect: if bread only was provided, it was almost certainly the family concerned who would decide whether it was to be white or brown.) Brown bread is preferable, and if it is to form a major part of the day's offerings it should be soaked so that it disintegrates and cannot be carried away by the larger and more aggressive birds. Perhaps the main value of bread is as a bait to induce those voracious species – Starlings, crows and gulls – to gather in the furthermost part of the garden, well away from the bird table. Broken biscuits can occasionally be bought quite cheaply and these, and stale cake, should be crumbled so that as many individuals as possible get a share.

A most valuable item in this section is oatmeal. The other cereals, wheat and barley, can be supplied whole, but birds seem to find considerable difficulty in dealing with the awns of oats. Fortunately oats are prepared in a number of ways for both human and animal consumption, and the birds are quite happy with all of them; so whether it be crushed oats such as one might feed to a pet rabbit or breakfast porridge oats matters little.

73

Breeding mealworms

A colony of mealworm beetles in a biscuit tin can provide thousands of larvae each month. For a breeding medium use two or three sequences of layers of coarse hessian/mixture of porridge or rolled oats and wholemeal flour/dry bran/dry stale bread. Introduce a few dozen adult beetles (for speed) or a few hundred larvae. Add a sliced raw potato once a week and make sure the lid, perforated finely for ventilation, fits well. The beetles lay eggs which hatch into mealworms, which pupate and emerge as beetles. Warmth (25°C/75°F) speeds up the process; cold slows it down. To harvest larvae insert a sheet of folded paper overnight – they collect in the folds. Renew the breeding medium when it has become a fine powder.

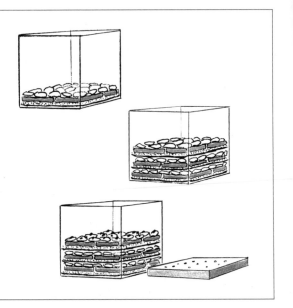

Live foods

Live food is not an essential item in the diet of those species which are likely to be in a British garden in winter, but they are relished by certain species – particularly Robins. Small quantities of mealworms can usually be purchased from the larger pet stores, but the dedicated bird feeder will probably want to establish his own stock. Maggots which are used by fishermen as bait can be obtained from fishing tackle dealers, but although cheaper than mealworms they are messy and not really satisfactory. 'Ants' eggs' (they are in fact the pupae) can sometimes be found in small quantities beneath stones or fallen logs.

Foods to avoid

Having dealt with the important categories of food which can be included in our birds' diet during the winter months we should now consider those which are either undesirable or even harmful. They are not numerous. Kitchen scraps which should be withheld include orange and lemon peel and banana skins. These, perhaps, are fairly obvious: much less obvious and far more dangerous is *any* substance containing salt. Salted peanuts must never be offered, neither must potato crisps or the rind from salt bacon. Any waste from highly spiced food should also be rigidly excluded. The best place for all of these is the dustbin – with the lid on. Fresh coconut is safe; desiccated coconut most certainly is not. Dry, it looks perfectly harmless, but once eaten it swells up in the bird's stomach with fatal results.

Water

The importance of water is covered in more detail in Chapters 2 and 8, but drinking vessels should certainly be topped up every time the food supply is replenished and kept free of ice during the hours of daylight in winter. Grit too is important. Since a bird has no teeth it digests its food by swallowing small particles of grit which pulverise the food in the gizzard. During periods of hard frost or when the ground is covered in snow a bird may be unable to find enough grit for its needs, and a supply on the bird table will be appreciated. The amount used will probably be quite small, so one of the packets sold for cage birds or a pound of the grit given to young chickens should be sufficient. As far as possible this should be kept dry; that on the bird table will present no problem if it is dispensed in a hopper, but the ground-feeding birds will also need a supply. The best solution is to put the container at the base of a wall, but once it gets wet it will inevitably freeze into a solid lump and become unavailable to the birds.

Cleanliness

Birds, like all other animals, are subject to disease and it is as well to remember that in the garden, and particularly at the bird table, we are harbouring them at a far greater density than is natural. It is a wise precaution, therefore, to scrub down the table at regular intervals with a disinfectant diluted to the level recommended by the manufacturer and to see that the food containers are thoroughly cleaned before being refilled. Feeding surfaces should ideally be impervious; wood can be made so by using a polyurethane seal. The ground beneath the table, too, is liable to become stale and soiled after a time, and if an alternative site can be found for it the table should be moved occasionally. The lawn as well as the birds will be the better for it.

Feeding birds is a growing hobby in Britain and the range of foods available is extensive. While it is unlikely that many new foods will come along, new techniques in presenting the food, or changes in the habits of the birds themselves as has recently happened in the cases of Siskin and Blackcap, may result in new species becoming regular visitors. Who knows? One day you may be able to emulate the Devon bird feeder who had the first Myrtle Warbler ever to be seen in Britain or Europe feeding at his bird table – on marmalade!

5 Birds to attract

The range of species

Newcomers to feeding birds in the garden will want to know what species they can expect to attract, while ardent bird gardeners will be keen to see how their efforts compare with those of others. One of the main aims of the Garden Bird Feeding Survey (GBFS) is to quantify the range of birds currently coming into gardens in Britain, and this chapter hopes to answer the questions likely to be posed by both new and experienced bird gardeners.

The GBFS was launched in the winter of 1970/71, and the findings from the first ten winters of observations form the basis of much of the information in this book. The project is simple: bird feeders are asked to describe and illustrate their garden feeding areas or 'feeding stations' on site registration cards (see p. 79). They then keep a weekly record over the six-month period from October to March of the peak number of each species coming to take food items artificially provided – an undemanding but engrossing task.

The organisers selected as wide a geographical spread of gardens as possible, to include city terrace dwellings, town flats and maisonettes, suburban houses and some rural homesteads so that all types of feeding stations were being watched each winter. The project was advertised in the daily press and bird journals, and received enthusiastic support; records from some 723 sites were received at some time over the first ten winters.

The survey soon demonstrated what a surprisingly wide variety of birds visit our gardens to eat foods artificially provided, with a staggering 117 species observed in the first ten winters (see p. 199).

Britain's most numerous owl, the Tawny Owl, occurs widely in many built-up areas as well as rural ones, wherever mature trees provide safe nest sites. In woodland its diet chiefly comprises small rodents, but in the garden it may swoop from a favourite perch in the apple tree at dusk or dawn to snatch small birds or fragments of meat and bone.

It also showed how the range of birds supported each winter can vary quite considerably from one garden to another. For example, during the course of the 1977/78 winter (which can be considered an 'average winter' for the decade as it had no prolonged cold or mild spells) the number of species taking food ranged from just 6 at a town garden in an urban part of Borehamwood, Hertfordshire, to an impressive 43 species recorded in a rural garden near Ottery St Mary, Devon. The number of species taking food in urban and suburban feeding stations ranged from 6 to 23 and at rural sites from 9 to 43; the average for the two habitats was 15 and 16 species respectively, showing how one can expect to attract a wide variety of birds even in town and city gardens.

In the following winter, 1978/79, arctic weather conditions had a sharp impact on both the numbers and range of species feeding in gardens; the average suburban garden supported 17 species and the average country garden 19 species, while the garden already mentioned at Ottery St Mary attracted 54 different types. This particular garden has a stream running though it, is bordered by moorland and scrub, and is very much designed with birds in mind but it shows just what can be achieved in a favourable place: such atypical garden visitors as Water Rail, Stonechat, Firecrest, Crossbill and Cirl Bunting came to take food.

Keep your eyes open for an unexpected visitor to the garden feeding area. The diminutive Firecrest (above) may come with a wandering tit flock for fat in country districts, while the seed-eating Cirl Bunting (below) is most likely to appear at rural gardens in the southwest peninsula where the nucleus of its dwindling population remains.

BRITISH TRUST FOR ORNITHOLOGY
Beech Grove, Tring, Hertfordshire.

OFFICE USE
ONLY PLEASE:

GARDEN BIRD FEEDING SURVEY   SITE REGISTRATION CARD   No. 007

Name of contributor: . G. H. GUSH . . . . BTO MEMBER? YES/NO

Address: . HIGHER METCOMBE, OTTERY ST MARY, DEVON . . . .

Address of feeding station
(if different from above) . . . AS ABOVE . . . .

Grid reference of defined area: Letters: S T Figures: 0 6 0 9 2 0

Description and history of the area. Please draw a sketch map of the defined area on the other side of this card and give some indication of the character of the immediate surroundings (see instructions).

Approximately how long has your garden been cultivated? . . 15 YEARS . . . . . .

Year (and month if recent) of start of regular feeding in your garden . . 1955 . .

Is your neighbourhood (area within 200 yards): URBAN/SUBURBAN/RURAL (see instructions).

Description (as concise as possible) of the 'DEFINED AREA',continue overleaf if necessary.

A LAWN SLOPING FROM THE HOUSE DOWN TO A SMALL MOORLAND TROUT STREAM, BOUNDED ON THE EAST BY A HERBACEOUS BORDER, BACKED BY A CREEPER — SHRUB COVERED FENCE & ON THE WEST BY A MATURE SLOTS

PINE TREE & CONCRETE PATH. THE COUNTRY BEYOND THE GARDEN TOWARDS THE SOUTH IS HEATHER/GORSE/ MOLINIA MOOR.

Members participating in the BTO's Garden Bird Feeding Survey are asked to complete a Site Registration Card giving on the front details of the location and history of the garden, and on the reverse a plan of the feeding area.

Frequency ratings

The list of garden birds coming to feed is dominated by a common 'top twelve' which were recorded at 60 per cent or more of the 723 feeding stations manned over the 1970s (see the table on p. 80). These species can be expected to appear at virtually any feeding station established in the country; they comprise three titmice, three thrushes, two finches, House Sparrow, Starling, Dunnock and, recent colonist, the Collared Dove. When ranked in order of frequency the Blackbird, Blue Tit and Robin top the lists each winter, feeding at 98 per cent or more of the sites, but when ranked in terms of the average weekly count at all feeders combined the House Sparrow and Starling appear as the most abundant feeding birds.

The 'top twelve' common garden feeders

Species	Relative Abundance		Frequency
	*Urban/Suburban**	*Rural**	*Percentage of sites where seen to take food*
Blackbird	2.8	3.2	99.3
Blue Tit	4.4	7.5	99.1
Robin	1.2	1.7	98.9
House Sparrow	18.7	14.3	96.6
Starling	15.5	10.1	96.4
Dunnock	2.1	2.6	95.2
Great Tit	1.8	3.6	93.0
Chaffinch	2.3	4.3	92.1
Greenfinch	4.1	4.8	91.5
Song Thrush	0.9	0.7	88.4
Coal Tit	0.6	1.2	69.8
Collared Dove	1.2	1.3	60.1

* Figures represent the mean weekly peak count

The 'local but often regular' feeders (taking food at 10–59% of the sites)

Species	Frequency
	Percentage of sites where seen to take food
Pied Wagtail	44.9
Mistle Thrush	34.6
Black-headed Gull	33.9
Wren	33.6
Jackdaw	32.4
Magpie	29.4
Rook	21.4
Bullfinch	21.0
Redwing	19.8
Great Spotted Woodpecker	19.6
Woodpigeon	19.3
Fieldfare	18.4
Nuthatch	17.9
Marsh Tit	17.0
Carrion Crow	15.6
Reed Bunting	13.5
Long-tailed Tit	11.4
Tree Sparrow	10.8
Jay	10.4
Brambling	10.3
Willow Tit	10.0

The 'scarce' feeders (taking food at 1–9% of the sites)

Species	Frequency
	Percentage of sites where seen to take food
Blackcap	9.7
Sparrowhawk	9.7
Common Gull	8.0
Siskin	7.3
Herring Gull	6.4
Yellowhammer	6.4
Feral Pigeon	6.1
Pheasant	5.9
Goldcrest	4.5
Moorhen	4.3
Grey Wagtail	4.3
Kestrel	3.9
Goldfinch	3.1
Lesser Redpoll	3.0
Treecreeper	2.2
Linnet	2.2
Mallard	2.2
Chiffchaff	2.1
Meadow Pipit	2.1
Lesser Black-backed Gull	1.3
Tawny Owl	1.3

The friendly Robin perching close by, looking for worms that have been dug up, is often the gardener's first close contact with local bird life.

When a film of ice covers the ground and vegetation, making natural foods unavailable, small birds like the Coal Tit (left) and Great and Blue Tits (below) will turn increasingly to man for alternatives. A well stocked bird table is therefore an important addition to any good bird garden. Putting out stored fruit will help those birds like the Redwing, seen opposite with Fieldfares, Blackbirds and Starlings, that are particularly susceptible to cold weather.

Nuthatches are relatively scarce except in rural gardens. They nest in small holes in tree trunks, as here, but Dutch elm disease has destroyed some natural nesting sites and garden nestboxes with small entrances are an acceptable alternative.

An old tree stump is not unsightly if a climbing plant is allowed to grow over it, and may well encourage the colourful Great Spotted Woodpecker. The much maligned ivy is useful to many species, for it supports nests and provides roosting cover, edible berries and insect-attracting flowers.

Few bird tables are without their conspicuous Robin in winter, but during the breeding season the bird can be elusive, cleverly concealing its nest in a building, cavity, or, as here, roofed over at the base of a hedge.

Goldfinches will raise two or three broods each year in garden shrubs. The neat, compact nest of this pair in the fork of a lilac has been partially flattened and decorated with faecal sacs by the well-grown young.

Suitably planted up with a variety of berry-bearing shrubs and coniferous trees for cover, a wild corner of the garden, seen here in summer (left) and autumn (right), becomes an attractive and valuable feature.

The pyracantha family (left) are important and versatile shrubs in the bird garden — they are used for nesting, roosting and food. Red berries are generally preferred by birds, but a notable exception is the evergreen Berberis darwinii *(right), whose long-lasting bluish purple berries are eaten by many species.*

Less widespread, often local (but sometimes regular) feeders include 21 species that took food at 10–59 per cent of all the feeding stations. These include certain birds which tend to be irruptive, such as the Redwing, Fieldfare, Jay and Brambling, appearing only when food supplies elsewhere have been exhausted. Also included in this group are several of the cold weather specialists which appear only in any great numbers in frost, ice and snow: such birds as the Scandinavian thrushes, Pied Wagtail, Tree Sparrow and Reed Bunting.

Another 21 species feeding at between 1 and 9 per cent of the feeding stations can be termed 'scarce', either through their limited range or the fact that they normally frequent an environment that most gardens cannot hope to mirror. For example the Pheasant, Meadow Pipit, Goldfinch, Linnet and Yellowhammer are essentially gregarious, flocking, open-country dwellers, while the Tawny Owl, Chiffchaff, Goldcrest and Treecreeper are primarily birds of closed woodland and the Mallard, Moorhen and Grey Wagtail specialist birds of waterside habitats.

An additional 65 species have taken food at less than 1 per cent of the 723 feeding stations observed during the 1970s. These include a number of species that are either very local or rare in status, such as the Lesser Spotted Woodpecker, Crested Tit, Hawfinch and Cirl Bunting. Others may have taken food perhaps more by chance or whilst on passage; among these are the Turtle Dove, Ring Ouzel, Wood Warbler, Spotted Flycatcher and Snow Bunting. Still more will resort to man for food only when conditions are extremely severe: the Grey Heron, Buzzard, Lapwing, Snipe, Kingfisher and Dipper (see p. 119).

Records abroad

The custom of feeding garden birds has increased in countries other than Britain, and interest in the GBFS has come from as far afield as Canada, Holland, South Africa and Australia. As sister schemes develop it will be interesting to compare the range of birds supported by feeders in different parts of the world. In Britain we may envy, for example, the Canadians for having the colourful Blue Jay as their most widespread feeder and for the regularity with which woodpeckers appear, but they in turn may not be quite so pleased with the abundant status that both the introduced House Sparrow and Starling have achieved.

Escapes

It is not unusual for a strange exotic species that defies all attempts at identification suddenly to appear at the bird table; such species

The price of freedom

As might be expected, the commonest escapees today are the Budgerigar and Canary, the species which are Britain's most common household caged birds. Most individuals will perish quickly through wind chill and starvation in the absence of adequate roosting cover or suitable food, though free-flying but homing flocks of Budgerigars have been established at intervals in several places with limited success. Other commonly kept cage birds like the Zebra Finch (right), Cut-throat and Cardinal may exist for a while under wild conditions, though usually with the support of man in the form of seeds taken from the garden bird table.

may be absent from even the most up-to-date of the field guides available. The great majority will prove to have escaped from a cage or aviary nearby. Not all escaped cage birds are necessarily doomed, though. If conditions prove suitable birds are quick to exploit them. The Ring-necked Parakeet is the most notable example today. This widely kept aviary parakeet of Indian and African origin is currently attempting to establish a viable wild population in Britain, seemingly with a degree of success. With the BTO's support Brian Hawkes has charted the spread of the bird over the recent decades. Ring-necked Parakeets have been observed in some fifty counties, from North Foreland in Kent in the east, to Newquay, Cornwall, in the west, and Wick, Caithness, in the extreme north. By 1980 pairs had been confirmed as breeding in at least ten counties, with concentrations in Kent, Surrey, Sussex, Essex and the Liverpool/Manchester area; the total population of Ring-necked Parakeets exceeds 1000 individuals.

Though the future of this small population is uncertain, individuals have proved themselves hardy to prolonged sub-zero temperatures as experienced during the severe winter weather of 1981/82. The Ring-necked Parakeet remains very much dependent on man, with 45 per cent of all records relating to gardens. A particularly aggressive species, it is frequently top of the 'peck order' at bird tables and is capable of driving off other species, including the Great Spotted Woodpecker and Nuthatch. Its diet comprises a large proportion of artificial foods (especially peanuts) but it also has a fondness for fruit of various types. Only time will tell if the Ring-necked Parakeet or other escaped species may exploit the foods we supply at our garden feeding stations.

Rare visitors

Throughout the main migration periods the alert householder may be delighted by the appearance of unexpected visitors to the garden. In spring species such as Redstart, Wheatear and Lesser Whitethroat in sparkling plumage are likely to be seen virtually anywhere, though usually stopping only briefly before pressing on to their breeding grounds. It is in the months of April and May especially that the fortunate bird feeder may glimpse a Black Redstart on the rooftop or a Hoopoe on the lawn – once seen, never forgotten!

Those warm, lazy, hazy days of autumn, however, are the best time for spotting birds on passage around the house. Annually from mid-July until mid-September, with stragglers into October, our summer visitors suddenly seem to find that gardens are worthwhile foraging sites. Fruit trees, soft fruit and runner beans may become alive, first with Willow Warblers, later with Chiffchaffs, signalling the prelude to actual emigration which may begin before July is out. Willow Warblers may show no preference between insects and berries at this time, but Lesser Whitethroats and Blackcaps reveal a marked taste for berries. With luck on his or her side the dedicated observer may be rewarded with 'garden birds of the year' just now, in the form of a Wryneck or Pied Flycatcher, even Bluethroat or Red-breasted Flycatcher.

Most small birds migrate by night, and when disoriented in bad weather exhausted birds drop into the nearest available cover, providing the garden birdwatcher with a welcome surprise. Having refuelled, this colourful spring Bluethroat will press on to its normal breeding haunts in Scandinavia.

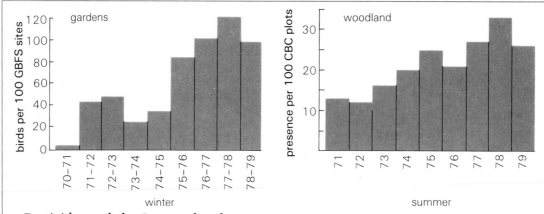

Pesticides and the Sparrowhawk

Organochlorine chemicals (and those of certain other pesticides) are typically concentrated along food chains, so that the top predator accumulates heavier concentrations of the pesticide than species further down the food chain. In these conditions Sparrowhawks suffered badly, partly through direct mortality but also because their breeding success was reduced. One of the effects of organochlorine poisoning in birds is to interfere with the production of the eggshell, so that Sparrowhawks (and other species) laid thinner eggs than usual. These eggs frequently fractured during incubation. Fortunately, the withdrawal of organochlorine pesticides from general agricultural use has led to a recovery of breeding success as the birds became able to lay eggs of normal shell thickness, and the Sparrowhawk has subsequently re-established itself over much of Britain. It is now not infrequently seen in the course of the winter visiting bird tables to snatch an unwary sparrow or other small passerine from the table for its own meal. As might be expected from a species with a history of persecution, Sparrowhawks are still quite rare in suburban and urban gardens, though even here there is some evidence since about 1976 of increased visits by Sparrowhawks in the course of the winter. The figure shows sightings of Sparrowhawks at (left) Garden Bird Feeding Survey sites in winter, and (right) Common Birds Census woodland breeding plots the following summer.

Comings and goings

Some of the birds now seen in gardens in winter have become relatively common only in recent years. The figure above left indicates the changes in the frequency with which Sparrowhawks, for example, have been sighted in rural gardens in the 1970s. Such increases could be due to a change either in behaviour or in real abundance in the country as a whole. In the case of the Sparrowhawk there has been a change in abundance, for the frequency with which it is sighted on the woodland census plots of the BTO's Common Birds Census scheme has also increased over this period (see above right). This recent increase is largely the consequence of the bird's recovery from the pesticide era of the 1950s, when organochlorine was used in seed dressings.

Since the first appearance of the Collared Dove (far right) in Britain in 1955 it has undergone a remarkable population explosion and is now a familiar sight in most gardens, cooing from the top of a fence or television aerial. The maps (right) show how rapidly the species has colonised Britain and Ireland. The current status is given on p. 6.

1955–56

1958

1961

1963

The Collared Dove is another species whose status has been changing in Britain and Ireland. The maps (left) give some indication of the spread of this bird from its first nesting in Norfolk in 1956, Scotland (Morayshire) in 1957, Ireland (Dublin and Galway) in 1959, and Wales (Cardiganshire, Pembrokeshire) in 1961, with other counties being colonised in between. By the time of the *Atlas of Breeding Birds in Britain and Ireland*, which was compiled during 1968–72, the birds had spread over much of the two islands, particularly around coastal areas.

This population increase is reflected in the greater number of Collared Doves appearing in gardens. The bird occurs predominantly in rural areas, though suburban gardens – except those near the centre of large cities – do have a good representation. No one knows exactly what has enabled the dove to spread as rapidly as it has. At the end of the nineteenth century the species was restricted to Turkey and the Balkans, but it has spread explosively since then: Hungary in 1932, Austria 1938, Germany 1943, Netherlands 1947, Sweden 1949, Belgium 1952, and Britain in 1955. Thus in the course of thirty years the bird has spread across the 1500 miles from Belgrade to the Outer Hebrides. It is a granivorous species which closely associates with poultry in farmyards, and it has clearly found a vacant niche or way of life for itself. These habits may well have pre-adapted it to using the winter food available on bird tables.

The Blackcap too seems to be increasing in Britain. The species normally winters in southern Europe and North Africa, but small numbers have long been known to winter regularly in Britain and there is some evidence that numbers have been growing since 1950. In 1945–54 there was an average of 22 birds recorded per winter (excluding November records), in 1970–77 the number was 380 per winter, while in the 1978/79 winter alone the corresponding number exceeded 1700. These changes are reflected by increasing numbers of Blackcaps found at suburban bird tables (see below).

The distribution of Blackcaps in the British Isles was surveyed in the winter of 1978/79 and they were seen to be more prevalent in the south-west, with other birds being found in Ireland. These are the warmer parts of the British Isles. Within these areas, too, the bird was found in the lowland regions, being increasingly scarce at higher altitudes. Unlike the Chiffchaff, another primarily summer visitor which has tended to increase in Britain in winter during recent years, Blackcaps are particularly numerous in suburban rather than in rural gardens. This is also linked with their willingness to take food at bird tables. Among foods observed being taken by Blackcaps have been bread (21 per cent of observations), fat (20 per cent), berries (16 per cent), apples (14 per cent), and peanuts (10 per cent). By comparison the Chiffchaffs wintering in Britain rely almost exclusively on natural foods in country areas and rarely feed at bird tables.

Why has there been such a big increase in the numbers of Blackcaps wintering in Britain? One reason must be the increase in Continental populations, since our birds originate from there. Blackcaps

Below: The figure on the left shows the increasing number of Blackcaps feeding at GBFS sites during the 1970s. The map on the right shows the distribution of sightings during the BTO survey winter of 1978/79.

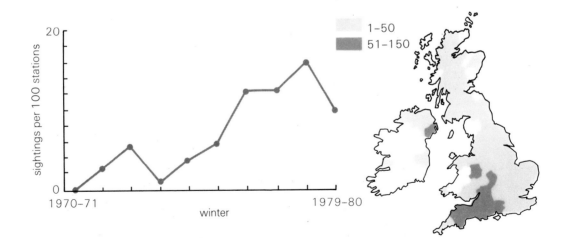

Watch out for the unexpected appearance of this delightful warbler, the Blackcap, on your bird table. Here a male is coming for fat, a favourite food. Blackcaps are bold, aggressive and able to hold their own against resident species up to the size of a Blackbird or Starling — probably another reason for their recent success.

are now from two to three times as common in Finland, Sweden and Norway as they were around 1950. However, a second factor must be the generally milder winter prevailing here nowadays: the average number of days with snow on the ground in the early morning in 1970–76 was half that for the period 1945–54, thus making it easy for wintering birds to find food on the ground. This must have been important for the Chiffchaff and probably for the Blackcap, though the latter's habit of feeding on bird tables may in any event make it less sensitive to severe weather.

The Sparrowhawk, Collared Dove and Blackcap are three of the most noticeable examples of birds that have come into gardens to feed more regularly and in higher numbers in recent years, but there are others too. Both the crow and gull families are proving to be remarkably adaptive groups, with representatives such as the Magpie and Rook, Black-headed Gull and Herring Gull including a higher proportion of foodstuffs from gardens in their diet. On a local scale observers have attributed the disappearance of former regular bird table visitors such as Nuthatch and Reed Bunting to clearance of woodland and drainage of wetland nearby, but the loss of these birds is more than made up for by the appearance of others including Siskin, Long-tailed Tit, Mistle Thrush and Kestrel. Indeed most of the signs indicate that our gardens are becoming increasingly important havens as feeding and breeding places for birds, and we can look forward to the company of an even wider spectrum of birds in the years ahead.

96

6 The foods different species like best

The Garden Bird Feeding Survey began during the winter of 1970/71, and the first winter was spent largely in establishing how feeding behaviour might best be recorded and what could be learned from the results. During the second winter (1971/72) observers were asked to record the food items provided and to group them under three headings for all birds as 'preferred', 'regular' or 'occasionally taken' foods. All participants were encouraged to use field glasses, but if they were still not sure of the food taken they were asked to indicate the probable item with a tick in the 'species' column. Since the quantity and variety of food varies considerably between gardens and a bias in favour of bread and peanuts was to be expected, so in the analysis of the food preferences of the thirty most regular garden visitors only the results from observers who had provided a full range of foods were included.

The comments below are based on returns from 620 observers from all parts of the country and from all types of feeding stations, in rural, suburban and urban habitats, supplemented by observations made in later winters. The birds are listed in the Voous order of classification, a system devised by the eminent Dutch ornithologist Professor K. H. Voous. This order has the advantage of drawing together birds of a similar type and is the sequence followed by ornithologists in publications today, including the most modern field guides available.

Ducks, geese and swans

Very few gardens can expect to attract waterbirds, though the Mallard is the most likely surprise visitor. However, any garden close to open water may quickly become a regular feeding ground for

The Siskin – a migrant from the conifer forests of northern Europe, is an exciting bird to see in one's garden. Its food preference in gardens today is peanuts in hanging orange nets, something it would never have seen in the wild. The peanut is a rich source of nutrition late in the winter when natural foods are becoming scarce and the Siskin needs to put on weight for its return flight to the breeding grounds.

duck once discovered, and numbers can then be expected to increase rapidly. Mallard will dabble or upend in shallow water for grain and come to the water's edge for bread and other scraps, and may be joined by Mute Swans, Canada Geese or more exotic wildfowl (see p. 199).

Hawks and falcons

Birds congregate wherever food is available, and birds of prey are no exception. If large numbers of birds gather around a feeding station, then sooner or later a Sparrowhawk or Kestrel is likely to become a visitor. The great majority of such aerial predators come to chase and kill small birds in and around the feeding area (as described in Chapter 10), but a few individuals have been seen to supplement their diet with meat and bones, even fat or suet.

Gamebirds

The Pheasant, and less often Grey Partridge, are most likely to visit secluded rural ground feeding stations and forage for grain. A few lucky observers have attracted feral examples of the Golden, Lady Amherst's and Reeves's Pheasants by presenting a variety of seeds.

Rails

Moorhens come to feed in a small number of gardens, taking mainly bread and corn from the ground. Having established the existence of a food source they often become regular visitors. Individuals may fly lazily up to feed from a raised table but this is not altogether out of character since Moorhens do spend quite a lot of time in trees and frequently nest and roost in them. Coot and Water Rail are rare garden feeders, coming chiefly to take scraps; the latter has a surprisingly aggressive habit of sometimes pursuing and killing smaller birds in the feeding area, usually during severe weather.

Gulls

The gulls are essentially scavengers, always on the look out for gatherings of their own or other species which might indicate that food is available. They employ two methods of feeding, either grouping in squabbling masses on the ground in open spots or, in confined areas, flying around and diving down to snatch the larger items of food which they carry away to a quieter place.

Most observations on food preferences amongst gulls were for the Black-headed Gull, by far the commonest garden visitor, fewer for Herring Gull and Common Gull, still fewer for Lesser Black-backed and Great Black-backed Gulls. Being opportunist feeders they were attracted by a wide range of foods: bread, obviously visible from a

Bird lovers in rural areas, with running water or a pond nearby, may be lucky enough to attract a Water Rail. This shy, skulking bird will venture cautiously from the cover of bushes, usually in the early morning or late evening, to jab at small fragments of food such as soaked bread before dashing back.

considerable height, meat, bones, fat, suet, fish, cheese, cake and potatoes – all were found acceptable, with perhaps a slight bias in favour of the bulkier items, although in one case even mixed seed was taken. All gulls are very aggressive when feeding, and few other birds are allowed to feed while they are around.

Doves

Collared Dove, Woodpigeon and Feral Pigeon are the three species most often noted, and by far the commonest of these is the Collared Dove. In all gardens the food preferred has been seed, grain or grain related foods – bread, cake etc., plus vegetable scraps. The Wood-pigeon occurs rather infrequently, and in suburban rather than rural areas. Its partiality to Brussels sprouts, beans and peas makes it an unwelcome visitor, and in country districts every man's hand is against it; in suburban areas and parks it is tolerated or even encouraged, and the flocks of Feral Pigeons in our largest cities often contain one or two which have discovered an easier way of making a living. All the doves are aggressive; the Collared Dove will drive away birds up to the size of a Jay or Magpie by rushing at them and battering away with its wings, while the Woodpigeon will tackle species up to the size of a Carrion Crow.

99

Kingfisher

A garden pond suitably stocked with minnows, sticklebacks, or the fry of larger species of fish may well repay you with close views of this brilliantly coloured bird. A perch in the form of a branch strategically positioned over shallow water helps.

Woodpeckers

Comparatively few feeding stations are visited by these birds though the number is increasing. All three of the British woodpeckers are strongly territorial even in winter, so only those birds whose territory embraces the garden are likely to use it at all regularly. It is important to present the food intended for woodpeckers in an easily accessible way – a wire container hung against the trunk of a tree is ideal – for although they will feed from the bird table or cling to hanging receptacles they are extremely nervous and the slightest movement behind an overlooking window will drive them away. Most bird tables are far too close to the house for their comfort. However, if the food is supplied some twenty yards from the nearest window the Great Spotted Woodpecker may quickly become a regular visitor, even bringing its newly fledged young into the garden where they will cling to any convenient trunk or fence post while awaiting the next meal.

The Green and Lesser Spotted Woodpeckers are even more reluctant to visit feeding stations, but the former may come for fat, fruit or mealworms, usually from the ground. The Lesser Spotted prefers peanuts or fat in a hanging container.

Larks and pipits

Especially during hard weather both Skylark and Meadow Pipit may come to eat bread crumbs, small seeds and wheat.

Wagtails

The Pied Wagtail is the one most likely to be seen around the garden, but in many areas its visits are irregular. During a spell of severe weather Pied Wagtails often become almost a permanent feature, paddling around industriously beneath the bird table picking up minute particles of food which are mostly invisible to the human eye, but the moment the weather improves they are apt to depart. A variation in the types of food taken at different times of the year has been noted; in both rural and suburban sites bread and seeds are commonly taken during the autumn, when a certain amount of insect food is probably still available, but in winter the Pied Wagtail favours fat, porridge or oatmeal – a more sustaining diet. Meat, biscuits and potatoes are taken occasionally.

The scarcer Grey Wagtail, normally a waterside dweller, appears in gardens infrequently in late autumn and winter to eat small seeds and fatty materials.

Waxwing

Waxwing invasions occur at irregular intervals and when they do the birds are likely to appear almost anywhere. They are particularly attracted to gardens, even in towns, where berries remain on the shrubs on house walls or in the open. Waxwings tend to flock, though individuals from a feeding party may leave to take water from the bird bath, or less often fruit or nuts from a raised bird table.

Wren

For so widespread a species it is surprising that this little insect-eating bird visits bird tables so very infrequently. Even when it does so it is just as likely to search the crannies around the roof or between the table and the pole for spiders and ignore the food supplied. It will sometimes take bread, small seeds, fat, minced peanuts and oatmeal, usually from the ground but occasionally from a table or a hanging container. Rural sites provide most records of individual Wrens becoming regular bird table visitors.

Wrens are constantly on the move in daylight hours to find enough food to satisfy their high energy needs in relation to their small body size, yet they suffer heavy mortality in long periods of freezing weather – more than two-thirds of our population perished in the severe 1962/63 winter.

Dunnock

Almost every feeding station has its Dunnocks, but they attract little attention, for this self-effacing species is happiest when shuffling around under the hedge or beneath the bird table, where it feeds largely on the fragments dropped by the birds feeding above. In summer the Dunnock is largely insectivorous, but in winter little comes amiss. It will take bread, although it rarely tackles the larger pieces, being content to clear up the crumbs which the larger birds ignore; all kinds of grain-based or farinaceous foods are acceptable, from breakfast foods to porridge, plus potatoes and small seeds. In rural sites it has been recorded taking meat, fat and fruit. Most of its feeding takes place on the ground, but just occasionally it can be seen on the bird table, usually when there are no other birds around.

Thrushes

Six species of this family are regular visitors to British feeding stations. In descending order of frequency of appearance these are Blackbird, Robin, Song Thrush, Mistle Thrush, Redwing and Fieldfare. In the summer and during mild winter weather most of these birds feed largely on worms and various larvae in grassland or in the debris beneath trees and shrubs, but in autumn they vary their diets with the berries of rowan and hawthorn and, later still, apples.

There is a difference in the feeding methods adopted by the larger thrushes. Mistle Thrushes and Fieldfares feed largely in open country, the latter often in flocks of considerable size, while Blackbirds, Song Thrushes and Redwings are usually to be found much nearer to the cover afforded by hedges and shrubberies, into which they can disappear when danger threatens. When the five species are brought into closer contact in the concentrated feeding area of the garden the Mistle Thrush is the dominant species, and at times it appears to spend so much time driving away the other thrushes as to leave little time in which to feed itself. In the absence of the Mistle Thrush either the Fieldfare or the Blackbird takes over the role of master of ceremonies, but skirmishes between rival Blackbirds rarely amount to much and if the food is scattered over a fairly wide area most of them seem to get a share. Song Thrushes and Redwings fare rather badly if any of the larger thrushes are present in the feeding area – as is usually the case – and since Redwings usually arrive only when weather conditions are particularly severe, every effort should be made to ensure that they manage to get something. The easiest way to achieve this is to throw an apple or two under the hedge or into the shrubbery well away from the main feeding area so that they are out of sight of the more aggressive species.

In cold weather individual Mistle Thrushes may become extremely possessive of local food sources, fiercely driving away smaller birds. Try to make fruit available to as many birds as possible by scattering it widely.

The Robin seldom comes into conflict with its relatives, and since Robins, whether male or female, hold winter territories they only show aggression towards any other Robin encroaching into that territory. This holds good for most of the winter, and it is usually only in exceptionally severe weather that the rule breaks down and Robins from neighbouring territories without feeding stations move in. In this case several may be found feeding together, but at the first sign of a thaw the old order is restored.

If the ability to adapt is the sign of a successful species the Robin will certainly succeed, for it eats almost anything. Bread is a preferred food, closely followed by seeds, fat, butter, suet, meat, fruit, vegetables and even peanuts. Oats, cheese, currants and cake are also liked, although mealworms top the list of the Robin's favourite foods: they are a prerequisite for anyone wishing to tame a Robin. In suburban districts Robins take most of their food from the ground, whilst in rural areas there is a more even balance. A few even manage to get food from hanging containers, either by hovering in front of it, grabbing a morsel and descending to the ground to eat it, or by clinging tenaciously to more stable feeders.

103

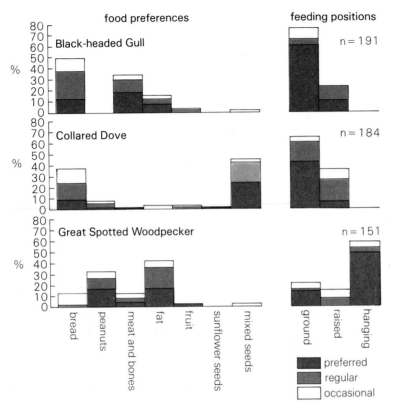

food preferences   feeding positions

Three species with very different major food preferences: Black-headed Gulls favour bread, meat and bones; Collared Doves like mixed seeds and bread; and Great Spotted Woodpeckers prefer fat and peanuts. Only the woodpecker is able to exploit hanging foods. On the charts on this page and on pp. 105, 106 and 107, 'n' represents the number of feeding stations at which observations were recorded over both halves of the winter.

In any list of garden visitors the Robin and the Blackbird are likely to appear in the top ten year after year. Like the Robin, the Blackbird will eat almost anything provided, adding only apples to the former's list. Individuals have even turned to the garden pond for small goldfish and other fish fry. Because Blackbirds prefer to feed in the open but like cover nearby, much of their food is taken on the ground; but tables are not ignored, and they sometimes fly at a hanging container in the hope of snatching a beakful of food.

The Song Thrush is a rather retiring bird, happiest when it can feed at a distance from its more pugnacious relatives. Its taste in food is varied and it is the only bird in this country to have solved the problem of how to extract a snail from its shell – which it does by battering the unfortunate mollusc on a stone. Sultanas, currants and cheese are highly favoured foods that can be given sparingly in the garden to gain the confidence of individual Song Thrushes, especially immatures in the autumn months.

Both Fieldfares and Redwings prefer to avoid man while there is food to be had in the open fields, but if conditions become hard both may eventually be compelled to seek sanctuary in the garden.

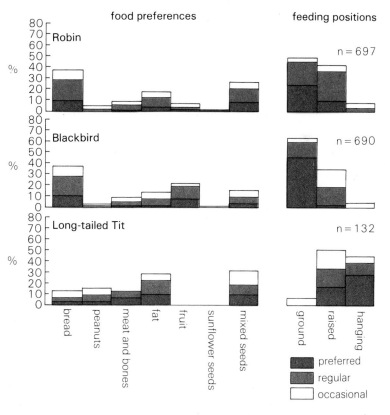

food preferences — feeding positions

Three resident species which have fairly catholic tastes at the bird table, although in the wild they feed very differently. Robins mainly feed on small invertebrates, and Blackbirds on large worms and fruit, while Long-tailed Tits pick at tiny food items from trees and shrubs. Robins and Blackbirds normally feed on or close to the ground; Long-tailed Tits most often high in the tops of trees.

Apples, in any state of decay, are a major attraction, and in orchards where the fruit of the trees grown as pollinators is allowed to fall unpicked, quite large flocks may occur. At one such commercial orchard a party of about 200 Fieldfares had almost cleared these windfall apples when it became apparent that some of the less popular varieties of apple in the cold store were unlikely to be saleable. They might have been dumped in an evil-smelling heap to encourage the local rats; instead, the tractor driver was instructed to fill up the manure spreader every other evening and scatter a load on a field of stubble. By the end of the first week the Fieldfare flock had grown to well over a thousand, and from then on it became impossible to count them with any accuracy. The field and the surrounding woodland swarmed with them. Some idea of the numbers can be gained from the fact that they were consuming a ton of apples every day, and at the end of each two-day period nothing remained but a few empty skins. Even the pips were taken, by Greenfinches and possibly Skylarks. It was noticeable that few Redwings appeared; those which did fed along the ditch beside the field, while a dozen or so Mistle Thrushes fed with the Fieldfares.

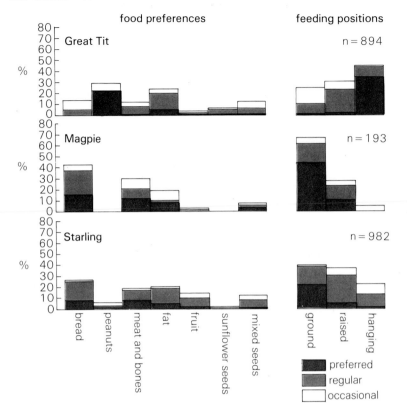

food preferences   feeding positions

Great Tits and Starlings are common and very adaptable visitors to bird tables. Each may take almost any sort of food and can cope with it on the ground, on raised tables or when suspended, though their preferred feeding positions contrast. Magpies are less frequent visitors to feeding stations and chiefly take bread, meat and fat; most are unable to cope with hanging food.

An unexpected garden feeder is always an exciting possibility, and the thrushes and their relatives are no exception. In rural gardens a Stonechat in winter may call in for seed, and the Black Redstart – a regular garden species on the Continent – may appear in urban areas during passage periods, attracted by meat, fat or fruit.

Warblers

Blackcap and Chiffchaff are two warblers which have overwintered in Britain and Ireland in greater numbers in recent decades, the Blackcap turning most often to bird tables for its food (see p. 94). The aggressive Blackcap, capable of dominating birds such as the Great Tit, Greenfinch and Robin on occasions, seems best equipped to hold its own in the feeding area.

Blackcaps eat mainly insects and berries in the autumn, but they come to the bird table in winter chiefly for bread, fat, dried fruit, peanuts and mixed seed. The full range of both natural foods (mostly berries) and bird table items was demonstrated by a BTO-aided survey organised by Ian H. Leach over the winter of 1978/79. In recent years Blackcaps have learnt to take fat and peanuts from

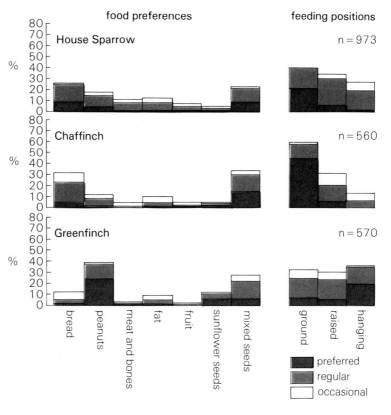

These three medium-sized seed eaters are all common at feeding stations and may take any sort of food on occasions. However, Greenfinches are clearly fonder of peanuts and sunflower seeds than are Chaffinches and House Sparrows, being equipped with larger and more powerful bills with which to handle these items. The smaller bill of the Chaffinch enables it to tackle smaller mixed seeds more successfully.

suspended baskets, initially hovering at the feeder taking a few pecks at a time, then clinging firmly, and some individuals feeding with tit-like agility.

Chiffchaffs stray less often from their basic insect diet, appearing only irregularly at bird tables for fat, meat, bread and other scraps.

Insects and spiders are the chief foods of the diminutive Goldcrest, but individuals may visit garden feeding sites regularly or on a casual basis when attached to tit flocks. They are fond of fat, cheese, peanut fragments and breadcrumbs, and will forage happily on the ground, from a raised table or a hanging container.

Tits

All seven species of British titmice appear at bird tables; in descending order of frequency of appearance these are Blue Tit, Great Tit, Coal Tit, Marsh Tit, Willow Tit, Long-tailed Tit and Crested Tit. All feed upon insects during the summer months, but in autumn and throughout the winter the first five turn largely to seeds of various kinds. In years when beech mast is plentiful this becomes an important item in the diet, more especially of the Blue, Coal and Great Tit,

107

until the crop is exhausted. At times the Blue, Great and Coal Tit move around in mixed flocks and these are frequently joined by a few Treecreepers, Nuthatches, Goldcrests, or in the autumn one of the smaller warblers. The lure of a well stocked bird table is often sufficient to persuade some individuals that there is nothing to be gained by wandering far from the garden.

All the three common titmice have very similar food preferences: peanuts are easily the most popular item, followed by fat, suet, coconut, cheese and sunflower seed. They prefer to take the food from hanging baskets or suspended by a thread, since this is their normal method of feeding when they are searching for insects in the outermost twigs of the trees. However, all three readily take food from bird tables, and will descend to feed upon the ground if there is food there or if the congestion around the feeding receptacles becomes too great. Blue Tit and Great Tit are avid milk drinkers, taking the cream from the top of milk bottles. Coal Tits are particularly given to hiding food and will spend much time carrying away peanuts or sunflower seeds; Great Tits seem to have caught on and will sometimes follow the Coal Tits and remove the hidden food the moment its rightful owner's back is turned.

Unlike the Blue and Great Tits, Marsh and Willow Tits rarely move far from their chosen territory, so in those stations fortunate enough to be able to record either species the same birds will probably appear day after day. Field identification is difficult – Willow and Marsh Tits are almost identical. Only in the song and in their nesting habits is there a marked difference, and both species are rather silent at the period when they are likely to be visiting the bird table. Their food preferences are much the same as those of the other tits, with peanuts, suet and sunflower seeds coming high on the list, and, like the Coal Tits, both are inveterate food-hoarders. They spend much of their time at shrub level, rarely frequenting the tops of trees as the Blue Tits do, but they are just as agile and have no difficulty in dealing with suspended food containers.

Long-tailed Tits are by choice largely insect eaters, industriously searching every twig for dormant larvae and pupae hidden in the crannies, and for this reason their numbers are severely reduced by prolonged spells of hard weather. Black ice, which covers all vegetation with an impervious glaze, is their worst enemy, and it is when this condition prevails that they may appear at the bird table. Having once done so, however, they may become quite regular visitors. Long-tails travel around in small parties, doing everything together; if one moves on to the next tree, they all move; if one settles on the bird table, they all do so. Oddly enough, although this is the smallest of the bird table visitors (if we exclude the tail), the sight of a dozen Long-tailed Tits around the edge of a feeding tray seems to have an inhibiting effect on the other birds, and they are usually allowed to stay until they are satisfied. Foods recorded include suet, meat, fat and peanut fragments, and less often bread. Tiny particles of food seem to be preferred, and melted fat poured on to a rough tree branch has proved popular. Grated cheese is also good, but is best placed on the bird table as Long-tails rarely feed on the ground.

The Crested Tit is a resident restricted to parts of north-east Scotland but it does visit nut hoppers and occasionally the raised table for various seeds, meat and fat scraps.

Nuthatch

In the autumn and winter this species feeds largely on hazel nuts, beech mast and the seeds of other trees. At this time it is largely arboreal, but when the trees have shed their crop it will search the ground below for the fallen seed which is taken back into the tree, wedged in crevices and hammered open. Although Nuthatches will sometimes join a winter flock of tits they do not flock with their own kind; pairs, however, seem to remain together so it is not unusual to see two birds at the table at the same time. Nuts – any sort of nuts – are its favourite food, but it is regularly reported as taking bread, sunflower seeds, cake, pastry, cheese, fat and melon seed, much of it from raised containers but also from the ground.

With its hard, dagger-shaped bill, powerful neck muscles and long, sharp claws the Nuthatch is superbly equipped to split and devour any nuts strategically jammed into the bark of tree trunks or logs in the garden.

The Treecreeper's adaptations — a fine, long, down-curved bill, long toes and sharp claws, and stiff tail feathers — enable it to exploit insect life in the bark of tree trunks.

Treecreeper

This is another species which, given the choice, is almost entirely an insect eater, finding most of its food in the crannies in the bark of trees. It is not a gregarious species but, like the Nuthatch, odd individuals will sometimes join a mixed flock of tits and in this way find themselves in the vicinity of a bird table. In the few gardens where Treecreepers do regularly take artificial food, fat, meat and bread are the commonest items, less often mixed seeds and crushed peanuts, sometimes from raised tables or hanging containers but more usually from baited rough bark tree trunks or stumps.

Corvids

All the crows are omnivorous. The larger species will take anything from the flesh of a dead rabbit or bird at the roadside to a freshly laid egg from the chicken run, and from fish which they take from the water while in flight to new potatoes which they dig for themselves. They are not therefore particularly welcome visitors to many bird gardens. The commonest visitor of the crow family to gardens throughout Britain is the Jackdaw, often coming in parties. In both country and suburban areas it will take bread, potato, fat, meat, fruit, peanuts and mixed seed — but as we have seen, nothing comes amiss, and whether the food is on the ground or on the table matters little. Even the food in hanging containers is not safe if the container will bear the weight of the bird.

The Magpie appears more frequently in rural sites than in the suburbs and its food preferences are similar to those of the Jackdaw.

The same can be said of the Jay. Most of the crows are rather nervous of man so their visits are usually confined to the early hours of the morning, and this applies particularly to the Jay. Nevertheless even when it is aware that it is being watched a Jay will dash from cover, grab the largest item of food in view and make for safety with a loud squawk of defiance. Crows are not easily discouraged.

The Rook and Carrion Crow are also more regular visitors to feeding stations in country areas and will consume virtually anything. Most of the food is taken from the ground, since only an oversize table will accommodate a Carrion Crow.

If one of your objects in feeding the birds is to record as many species in the garden as possible you will have to include the members of the crow family, but their presence will most certainly discourage some of the smaller birds, and efforts can be made to limit their visits. Perhaps the best way to achieve this is to see that the food is always supplied in small pieces and that it is within sight of a window. Few crows will tolerate the presence of a human figure less than twenty yards away.

Starling

During the winter months Starlings feed in compact flocks, constantly searching the ground and probing with open mandibles for worms and other invertebrates. They also take large quantities of fruit, both wild and cultivated, in season. They are frequent visitors to the bird table, but their voracious appetites and aggressive habits often make them less than welcome. It is not so much that they will eat anything – they invariably eat everything, so that the question of food preference is hardly relevant. For the record, the items most commonly taken are bread, meat, fat, bone marrow, fruit, chicken flesh, pastry, cheese, minced peanuts, mealworms, coconut, oats, rice, sultanas, porridge, creamy milk, peanut butter and dried figs. If anything else is offered, that no doubt will be accepted too. Although most at home on the ground, Starlings feed happily on raised surfaces and are not easily defeated by most hanging containers. They are remarkably versatile birds.

Sparrows

The House Sparrow and the Tree Sparrow are two contrasting visitors to feeding stations. In suburban areas the former is one of the most regular guests. There are, however, still a few rural areas where House Sparrows are reported rarely, most of them in areas remote from towns and villages. During the winter months rural House Sparrows feed mainly on the ground, often in large flocks, on grain and weed seeds, while their urban and suburban relatives rely largely on the waste from human households. These are the birds which profit most from those good people to whom feeding the birds means scattering the crusts and crumbs from the breakfast table on to the lawn.

The House Sparrows give something in return for, especially when feeding their young, they may often be seen meticulously searching the lower branches of shrubs and the underside of leaves for aphids and small green caterpillars. At the bird table, however, they are apt to forget their winning ways and, like Starlings, they will quickly dispose of almost everything in sight, whether on the ground, on the table or in a wire container. Peanuts and bread are particularly favoured, but there is scarcely anything which is likely to be offered which they refuse. It is tempting to suggest that the House Sparrow is too successful because it groups in large gangs, tends to exclude other species and is wasteful in its feeding habits.

In sharp contrast, Tree Sparrows occur much less frequently at bird tables, are relatively shy and when they do appear it is usually in country areas or on the outskirts of villages. During the winter they often collect in large flocks, sometimes with finches of a variety of species, when they feed on weed seed in neglected root fields or on rubbish tips and waste ground. In the garden they are attracted chiefly to mixed seed, peanuts and bread and will also eat meat and fat, most often from the ground but also from hanging baskets and bird tables.

Finches

Ten species of finch may be expected at bird tables or feeding stations at various times. These in order of decreasing frequency of appearance in most years are Chaffinch, Greenfinch, Bullfinch, Brambling, Siskin, Goldfinch, Redpoll, Linnet, Hawfinch and Crossbill. Finches can be divided into three groups: those which feed mainly on the ground, those which feed largely from vegetation and those which feed both on the ground and in vegetation, including trees.

So we find the Chaffinch and the Brambling which gather their winter food, mainly seeds and fallen tree fruit, on the ground, the Greenfinch, Linnet and Redpoll feeding both on the ground and by clinging to plant stems while extracting the seed from pods or capsules, and the Goldfinch and Siskin feeding mainly in trees on the seeds of alder or birch, or on the seeds of composite flowers such as thistle or teasel. There is a certain amount of overlap, however; the Redpoll feeds extensively on both birch and alder seed and would appear to fit into the group with Goldfinch and Siskin rather better than it does with Greenfinch and Linnet. The Bullfinch falls into a

112

The delightful Chaffinch appears in our gardens all year round and will be happy with grain-based foods like bread, as well as with peanuts and seed. With patience, individual birds may become very tame and take food from your hand.

separate category, feeding mainly on buds, tree flowers, berries and the softer, often half-ripe seed heads of dandelion, chickweed, ragwort, etc. Both the Hawfinch and Crossbill feed mainly high in trees, taking kernels and cones before extricating the seeds.

Not surprisingly it is the ground and near-ground feeders which occur most frequently at feeding stations, but the Siskin, a largely arboreal species, has in recent years adopted the habit of visiting bird tables for peanuts and fat, often appearing in considerable numbers.

One possible reason why three of the species which might be expected to be attracted by seed – the Goldfinch, Linnet and Redpoll – are infrequently found in gardens is that they are essentially flocking species. Where they appear there is usually an extensive feeding area of weed seed, and a large flock of birds can work the area for a considerable time. These flocking species may not be interested in the relatively tiny feeding areas which garden bird feeders are able to produce.

113

Of the finches which do patronise gardens the Greenfinch is the most likely to be influenced by the type of food supplied. If peanuts or wheat are offered there will be Greenfinches; if they are not, there will invariably be none. This is not to say that Greenfinches eat nothing else. They will take sunflower seed, mixed seed (which may well contain both wheat and sunflower seed) and even such mundane items as bread, cake and fat, but the nuts and wheat are the main attraction.

Chaffinches feed largely on the ground and only a few of the more regular visitors make use of the bird table at all frequently. Mixed seed is preferred, but it is usually only the smaller seeds in the mixture which appear to be taken regularly, although sunflower seeds are sometimes eaten. Oats, either crushed or of the refined and processed variety, are taken; also, in much smaller quantities, bread, fat, cheese, potatoes and apple seeds. In recent years a few Chaffinches and Bramblings appear to have learnt that food may be obtained from hanging containers, but their attempts to emulate the Greenfinches and tits have met with limited success.

In many gardens Bullfinches, although constantly present in and around the garden, appear consciously to shun the bird table and feeding area. Small seeds, especially rape, fruit and rather surprisingly breadcrumbs are the usual items eaten. Bramblings are attracted to oats, mixed seed, bread and fat, and Goldfinches to fine seed and peanut fragments taken mainly from the ground but occasionally from raised tables and rarely from suspended baskets.

Siskins arrive very irregularly; in some winters they are plentiful, in others there are few. In the feeding area they will take peanuts, fat (especially that allowed to hang for rather too long), cheese, coarse oatmeal and seed, and how or where the food is presented appears to make little difference to the birds. Linnets are rarely to be seen eating artificial food, and then it is usually small seeds of grains and grasses. Redpolls may come to take mixed seed, but in dry areas they are more likely to be attracted to water.

Both Hawfinch and Crossbill are heavy billed finches which may first be tempted to drink and bathe at the garden watering place. Having discovered a source of water they may turn their attention to the bird table. Hawfinches will come shyly for dried fruit, large seeds and peanuts; Crossbills may become tame in time, small parties visiting bird tables for seeds, especially sunflower seeds and peanuts.

Many of the finches will adopt a threatening attitude towards other birds when they are feeding, and the Siskin appears to be particularly antagonistic towards birds with yellow in their plumage — tits and even Greenfinches are sometimes attacked — but the threatening behaviour rarely results in serious trouble.

Despite having distinctive plumages both Corn Bunting (left) and Reed Bunting (right) often go undetected among the wintering flock of seed eaters beneath the bird table. Their arrival usually coincides with a hard frost or snow, but once established, individuals may patronise a site on and off before dispersing as late as early April.

Buntings

In descending order of likely appearance Reed Bunting, Yellowhammer and Corn Bunting are the three species that may be attracted to the garden feeding area. Yellowhammer and Corn Bunting are essentially seed eating birds of open country which sometimes appear at exposed rural feeding sites taking any corn, weed seeds or dried fruit scattered on the ground. Somewhat surprisingly it is the Reed Bunting, primarily a bird of wetlands, which arrives in gardens most frequently, even appearing in suburban situations during hard weather conditions, when it is partial chiefly to mixed seeds. It will also take pastry, bread and cake, sometimes even venturing from the ground on to the raised table.

7 Numbers of birds in our gardens

How many birds take advantage of the food supplied at a bird table? At first sight this question requires only the simple counting of birds coming to the table, but in practice estimating the number of individuals of the various species which are taking food in the garden can be difficult. One ringer described his experiences with Long-tailed Tits thus:

> Early one January a flock of ten arrived at the bird table and lined up around its rim to feed on grated cheese. When they had gone, a circular wire trap with a dished wire lid (like an inverted dustbin lid) with a circular hole in the centre was placed in the apple tree and baited with more cheese. After several excursions to remove unwanted Blue and Great Tits, patience was rewarded and the Long-tails returned; all ten entered the trap and were ringed and liberated, care being taken to see that they were all released together so that the flock should remain intact. For the next few days the visits continued, but always to the bird table, never to the trap, and the sight of ten Mumruffins with their shiny rings decorating the edge of the feeding tray became quite commonplace. And then, one morning, there were only six on the table, each bearing a ring, but there were four more in the trap, all unringed. This was rectified, but the following day it happened again and three more birds collected rings. By the end of the winter 26 Long-tailed Tits had been ringed, all from the same trap in the same tree, and the apparent size of the flock visible at any one time in the garden had never exceeded ten birds.

Other species have yielded even more striking examples of the difficulties of counting. In one garden in Tring, not far from the BTO

The Redwing, an attractive small thrush, is mostly a winter visitor to Britain although a few pairs breed in northern Scotland. Its numbers vary greatly from year to year, and most of those that reach Britain feed in the countryside, largely on the berries of hawthorn, rowan, holly and yew. However, as soon as the weather becomes really cold they may become familiar, tame visitors to gardens throughout the country.

offices, a careful Garden Bird Feeding Survey count produced a maximum of nine Blue Tits at the feeding station at any one time during the week. Yet in a single day's catching a total of 148 different Blue Tits were ringed there. In fact, experienced bird ringers find that they typically catch ten times as many Blue Tits in a garden as are actually recorded there at any single moment. Greenfinches are even more misleading in this respect: in some gardens the largest winter flock recorded has been of about 40 birds, but more than 1000 different individuals have been ringed there.

The Long-tailed Tits mentioned above differ from most British titmice in remaining largely insectivorous over the winter. During this season they form small flocks (6–30 individuals), with few birds ever moving from one flock to another. Individual flocks defend territories and eject intruding birds, though two or more flocks may overlap in range near the boundaries. In one Oxfordshire study, individual birds within flocks were found to spend about 90 per cent of their daylight hours feeding in February, and it is at this time of year that most Long-tailed Tit flocks are to be seen feeding at garden bird tables. Presumably this is the time that the birds are most hungry. Display and nest site investigation begins in March when small insects become available again, and most Long-tailed Tits using gardens move back into woodland at this time. Why do tits not breed in gardens, relying on food from the bird table? Obviously some birds do just this, and their territorial behaviour prevents others using that food. But also, many gardens lack dense vegetation and holes used for nesting by these species, which are forced to return to the woodland to find vacant nest sites even though they must then wait for the insects to reappear. In fact many territorial woodland birds engage in brief periods of territorial display in the woods for part of each day in late winter and early spring, returning to the gardens to feed, particularly when the weather turns cold. A Swedish scientist tested this explanation by bringing bird tables into the wood and feeding birds there. Great Tits in whose territory he set up a steady supply of artificial foods subsequently bred earlier than did birds without a feeding station in their territory.

Seasonal trends

Different species of bird come into gardens at different times of the year: some of the patterns observed are shown on p. 120. Several small birds such as Wrens sharply increase their use of the artificial food supplied at bird tables during the months of October and November, but their attendance decreases through the rest of the year. In some cases the decline is due to mortality: small birds have to metabolise their food so intensively in order to survive at low

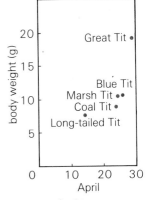

As insect food increases each spring small birds such as Long-tailed Tits more quickly find enough food to enable them to lay their small eggs than do larger birds such as Great Tits that lay bigger eggs. Small resident species therefore usually breed earlier than do larger species.

118

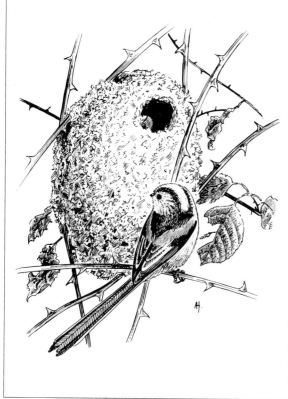

The early bird ...

March may seem a surprisingly early date for our small birds to resume breeding, but this is part of a general pattern for titmice (left, Long-tailed Tit). With the warmer weather insects and other invertebrates reappear in woodland – in small numbers and of the hardier species at first, more abundantly and with extra species later in spring. Since small birds lay small eggs, they need less food over and above their basic existence requirements to allow them to form their one egg per day, and so can start breeding before the spring flush of insects is fully under way. By the time their young hatch a couple of weeks later there is an abundant supply of food available for rearing the nestlings and of course for the young fledglings while they make their precarious transition to independence. The larger titmice must wait until the food supplies have risen enough to allow them to form their larger eggs, and their young therefore miss the peak of food abundance. Comparison of GBFS results for the different titmouse species shows a tendency for the larger species to remain, feeding at bird tables later each spring because they cannot start breeding in woodland.

temperatures that even a small period without food – for example, due to a spell of wet weather, to competition from larger birds feeding at the table, or to the arrival of a predator in the garden – can quickly deplete their condition to a fatal level.

Larger birds are not immune to winter, either. Midwinter days are shorter than at other times of the year, so even if temperatures also were not decreasing at this time, birds would have to search more intensively for food during the day in order to have enough fat reserves to live on through the longer night. This affects large and small birds alike, and the GBFS results show some species such as the Magpie coming into gardens with maximum frequency in December, when days are shortest.

A third category of birds coming to the garden might be described as 'cold weather specialists'. A good example here is the Black-headed Gull, which most frequently appears at feeding stations in late January and February, which are the coldest months of the year. In Britain, the winter climate trends are such that the temperature lags slightly behind the sunshine curve: the lowest temperatures are

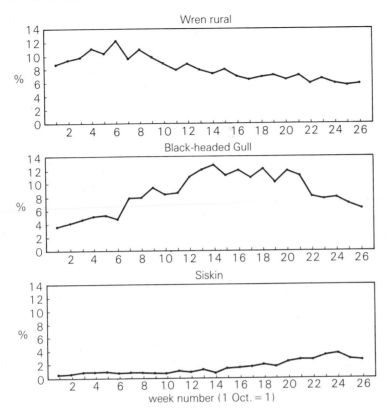

Wren rural

Black-headed Gull

Siskin

week number (1 Oct. = 1)

Some typical trends in the presence of birds at garden feeders, October to March. The vertical axis shows the percentage of gardens with the appropriate species present, for (above) a species whose members die throughout the winter (Wren), for (centre) a cold weather specialist (Black-headed Gull), and for (below) a scarce species using gardens only after natural foods are exhausted (Siskin).

reached about a month after the period of least sun and the warmest temperatures are attained about a month after maximum sunshine. This lag in the heating and cooling of the earth is due to the storage of heat at the earth's surface and its gradual release to the atmosphere later. For this reason species that are affected by freezing conditions experience their food shortage in January and February rather than in December and consequently appear at bird tables in greater numbers in those months.

Natural food supplies

For several species the supply of natural food declines seasonally, so that food is scarcest in late winter, before spring growth renews the food supply. Species of this type, such as the Bullfinch, consequently increase in attendance at artificial food sources until quite late in the winter. Bullfinches in winter subsist almost exclusively on the seeds of two types of herbaceous plants, dock and nettle, two shrubs, bramble and privet, and two trees, birch and ash. As these seeds become scarce at the very end of winter, the main diet available to the birds consists increasingly of buds. However, feeding trials of

120

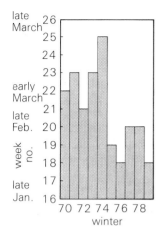

late March 26
25
24
23
early March 22
21
late Feb. 20
19
18
late Jan. 16 17
week no.
70 72 74 76 78
winter

Above: The general trend during the 1970s was for Greenfinches to come into gardens at increasingly early dates, reaching winter peak numbers in weeks 22–23 in 1970/71, but doing so six or seven weeks earlier (week 18) by 1979.

During recent decades, as farming methods have changed, Greenfinches have been appearing at garden feeding stations earlier and in larger numbers each winter. Typical of the species, this cock bird preferred peanuts and sunflower seeds.

captive birds have shown that in winter Bullfinches cannot maintain their weight when feeding on buds alone, irrespective of the species of tree concerned: they must have some seeds in order to survive. By the end of February, however, when buds are larger and days longer, the birds are able to exist on buds. This is reflected in the trends of attendance by Bullfinches at garden feeding areas: peak attendances are just before the natural food supplies become more tolerable again.

Greenfinches, too, undergo seasonal changes in the balance of their diet. The large beak of the Greenfinch enables it to take a wide variety of foods, with larger seeds being preferred. When these birds are on farmland charlock and persicaria provide a high proportion of the winter food. They also take many grains from stubble fields but hardly touch the smaller seeds of wild grasses. Dr Ian Newton, author of the classic monograph on finches, points out that in the past Greenfinches regularly assembled at stackyards and threshing

places during hard weather, though with the advent of the combine harvester in most areas this habit has died out. Instead, the birds move into towns and villages in cold weather: during the extensive frost of January–March 1963, Dr Newton found that an astonishing 97 per cent of the volume of all food taken by Greenfinches consisted of peanuts!

Greenfinches have become more regular feeders at bird tables since that time: even over the ten-year timespan of the GBFS they have been coming in earlier each year to feed at bird tables. The average expectation of life of an adult Greenfinch is three years, so a significant proportion of the population alive each winter will have fed the previous year at bird tables. Such birds would be more likely to remember these food sources as natural feeding gets more difficult each winter. Another factor may be the increased use of pesticides on farmland. Agricultural spraying programmes are designed to reduce the amount of weeds growing on arable land and, if successful, must reduce the level of natural foods available to Greenfinches, causing them to prolong their earlier use of artificial foods. The importance of artificial feeding for the survival of Greenfinches in the absence of natural foods is emphasised by the Garden Bird Feeding Survey finding that the number of breeding Greenfinches on farmland was generally greater in years in which larger numbers of feeding birds were recorded on suburban bird tables during the previous winter.

Changes in natural food supply also seem to affect the abundance of Coal Tits feeding at bird tables. Coal Tits are insectivorous in summer but in winter take a considerable amount of seeds, feeding especially on oak, ash and beech trees (though in some cases they are taking insects from these trees). Production of tree seeds tends to follow a biennial pattern: if there is a good seed crop one year the trees require something akin to a rest year the following season. The relationship is not exact, however, and two poor years are quite likely to follow one another. Something of this periodic boom and bust in natural foods can be seen in the GBFS data for Coal Tits at feeding tables in Britain (see p. 123). Bird table foods are seen to be taken most readily when natural foods normally preferred by the birds are not available.

Much the same story emerges from a study in Holland of the use made of beech nuts by Great Tits in woodland there. The fall of beech nuts in Holland occurs mainly in October. These nuts at first merely accumulate on the floor of the forest, but from late October onwards they start dwindling in number until by February there is only about 10 per cent left. This decrease is due to predation by birds, mammals and insects. In Holland the earliest consumption of

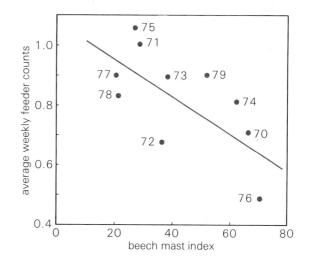

Beech mast is a valuable winter food of several small woodland birds, including the Coal Tit. The crop varies considerably from year to year but can be assessed using an arbitrary scale: 20 = very poor, 40 = moderate, 60 = fairly good, 80 = very good. (Data from Dr J.H. van Balen.) The number of Coal Tits coming to take food provided on bird tables each winter decreases in proportion to the amount of beech mast and other natural foods available.

beech nuts is by Chaffinches and Bramblings, but from around mid-November Great Tits, Blue Tits, Marsh Tits and Nuthatches are also observed feeding under the beech trees. The tits feed on the beech nuts principally on cold days. In England beech mast falls rather later than in Holland, mainly in November and December, and Great Tits spend an increasing proportion of the time feeding on the ground from September through to March and April. The availability of beech mast has a big effect on the survival of juveniles up to November/December, with the rate of immigration into the wood depending partly on the size of the crop.

Peck orders

Whenever food is limited flocks of feeding birds appear to develop 'peck orders' or dominance hierarchies. In the simplest form of these hierarchies one particular bird is dominant over all other conspecifics (birds of the same species) in the flock: a second bird is dominant over all conspecifics except the top bird; a third bird is dominant over all except the top two birds; and so on. In such hierarchies males frequently outrank females and adults outrank juveniles. Great Tits seem to form peck orders in autumn, and it is often the inferior first-year birds that leave the woods to seek food elsewhere. In a Dutch study the early arrivals in autumn and early winter at feeding stations at the edge of the wood were predominantly juveniles, with adult birds appearing only later in more severe weather conditions. It is likely that the same is true in Britain: early arrivals at the bird tables are probably juvenile birds, with adults appearing later.

123

One of the principal advantages of a peck order is that the birds involved 'know their place' in the flock and avoid wasting time in disputes whose outcome is already predictable. Many interactions within such flocks involve subordinate birds which move away at the approach of a dominant one. This obviously makes life fine for the dominants, but the subordinates too will be better off in a low status position within the flock than in an independent life outside it. Many of the species that flock in winter take food that occurs in clumps and is thinly spread elsewhere. A subordinate bird would thus have to spend a great deal of time searching for such food if it were to leave the flock.

Birds like the Greenfinch, which congregate in flocks, squabble continuously. Here a dominant bird refuses to allow a subordinate to gain a foothold. Established flock members often feed peacefully in the background. Provide for them all by not putting all the food in one place.

Any form of peck order involves a degree of status recognition among flock members. At first sight individual recognition of flock members might be thought necessary, and it probably is common among flocking birds, but there are other possibilities. An army sergeant is recognisable to a corporal as being of higher status simply because he wears three stripes as against two, even though the men may be complete strangers. Likewise, few people would argue with a queue-jumper who had the build of a heavyweight wrestler. Something similar probably occurs among Great Tits, for dominance status in winter flocks has been shown to be linked to body size, bigger birds being of higher status.

An interesting example of status marking has been shown to exist in an American species called the Harris Sparrow (actually more closely related to buntings than to sparrows). This species forms winter flocks in which marked hierarchies exist on the basis of the amount of black (or brown) in each bird's plumage: the more black present, the greater the bird's status in the hierarchy. It seems probable that the degree of blackness is linked to the level of testosterone (or one of the related male sex hormones) and thus to fighting ability, but in any event most Harris Sparrows do not wait to argue with a very black individual approaching them – they move away promptly! Subordinate individuals also maintain a respectful distance around the blacker individuals.

Experiments such as the one described on p. 126 provide fascinating insight into how birds in a flock regulate their affairs, but they also have a message for the garden bird feeder: artificial foods spread out over several tables or at a variety of points in the garden will benefit more birds than will the same foods concentrated into a single heap.

Hoarding of food

One alternative (or supplement) to a bird maintaining its position in a hierarchy is for it to remove as much food as it can from the clump and hoard it elsewhere for private consumption. Several of the common species at the bird table – most especially Coal Tit and Nuthatch – are regularly to be spotted doing just this.

Hoarding is likely to occur whenever a food is temporarily abundant and unavailable outside this period. It is also especially likely if the birds encounter a surplus when hungry or under pressure to find food, for example when busy collecting food for hungry nestlings. Captive Ravens were found to hide more food away the longer they had been kept without. Moreover, they hid the more nutritious food with the best keeping qualities, such as fat and fatty meat – a point of relevance to the habits of Coal Tit and Nuthatch who will

Wearing the right uniform

What happens if the status markings of an individual bird are altered so that birds have the inappropriate markings for their rank? Two American scientists tried just such an experiment, with fascinating results. Dominant birds whose black markings were bleached to a lower rank spent a great deal of time attacking subordinates, apparently because these latter no longer kept the same distance from the dominants as they used to. At one level, then, the bleached bird found himself living in a disrespectful world, to his fury. More likely, though, is the explanation that such birds regarded their previously guaranteed access to food threatened by increased frequency of approach by flock members and consequently thought more aggression was called for. In the same experiment subordinate birds were dyed blacker, to a higher ranking, but they too had a rough time in the flock. Instead of being treated with greater respect they were actually attacked far more than they were as subordinates. Not 'knowing' of their new status badges they of course continued to behave as subordinates, moving away at the approach of dominants. Such inappropriate behaviour was perceived by flock mates as indicating that a previously dominant bird was ill or otherwise incapacitated, thus providing an ideal opportunity for gaining an increase in their own relative status. The American ornithologist describing these results called this phenomenon 'kicking the tough guy when he is down'.

The head and throat markings of six Harris Sparrows, showing variation in the amount of black from one bird to another. (From S. Rohwer and F.C. Rohwer, 1978, Anim. Behav. 26, 1012–1002.

remove peanuts and sunflower seeds for storage in preference to other foods on the bird table. It would be interesting to know if Coal Tits store food most intensively on cold days when their needs are greatest and they are likely to be especially hungry.

Jays are regular hoarders of acorns, especially in September and October, and in years with poor crops they have been recorded collecting them over distances of as much as 1.2 km. The Jays do not push the acorns into the ground at random, but store them in the vicinity of saplings which appear to serve as markers. To relocate the acorns, the birds hunt for newly germinated saplings, pulling them up and eating the acorns from which the saplings sprang. The older saplings, which originally acted as markers and will have used up the food reserves in the acorn, are rarely sought by the Jays.

Marsh Tits and Willow Tits appear not infrequently at bird tables in Britain during the course of the winter, and, with Coal Tits, are among the most frequent species observed to carry away food from the tables to hoard in hiding places elsewhere. Indeed, at times one gets the impression that hoarders like Coal Tits avoid the hurly burly of the bird table, hanging back until a quiet period at the table occurs and dashing in to remove a peanut and carry it away to secrete it elsewhere. This behaviour is useful if the birds have a surplus of food available to them at one time of the year, the food cache then supplementing their diet when times are harder.

Studies with marked peanuts and colour-ringed Marsh Tits have shown that individual birds remember where they have hidden food items and subsequently recover them. Not all hidden items are recovered by the owner: some are 'pirated' by other tits which find them in the course of their normal search for food. It therefore obviously pays the birds to ensure that as few conspecifics as possible have the opportunity to search in the area for food. Willow Tits and Crested Tits in Sweden have been shown to have resolved this problem by dividing their habitat up into group territories defended by three to four birds. Most territories were defended by a pair of adult Willow Tits, though one or two juvenile birds (not their offspring) were allowed to join them. These small groups defended their territory against groups of conspecifics, thus ensuring a minimum chance of strangers getting at the hoarded food. Naturally, there is a risk that within each group individuals might steal food previously stored by group members, but this seems to be avoided by differential use of the resources within a group territory. If birds normally search in slightly different parts of their habitat and tend to store their own hoarded food in such parts they will not come across each other's food stores very frequently, so little theft occurs.

One might well ask why the adults do not defend the territory exclusively, particularly when the adults present are usually a pair from the previous breeding season. One reason may be that many adults will lose their mate in the course of the winter because of the high mortality rate experienced by these small birds. If this happens, they can readily find a new partner among the first-year birds they have allowed to share the winter territory. In one study eight out of every ten such replacement mates came from within the winter social group. However, adults can also minimise the extent of food competition through aggressive behaviour towards the first-year birds. The older, more experienced, adults usually dominate first-year birds.

A Jay eating an acorn, which this species regularly hoards in the autumn.

127

Conversely, there must be some advantages to the first-year birds in settling into a territory already possessed by an adult pair. Early settlement by Willow Tits is highly desirable if they are to store enough food in the autumn and early winter before it gets scarce. At this time of year most of the available territories are occupied by breeding pairs, and there are few complete vacancies available for the first-year birds. In addition there may be advantages in teaming up with adults, such as learning what foods to take or where to look for food. It may also help the first-year bird avoid predation.

Influxes of birds

Every few years, rather irregularly, unusually large numbers of Fieldfares and Redwings move out of Scandinavia and into the British Isles in search of food. This type of irruption, as it is called, takes place also in the case of other northern forest birds such as the

The appearance in winter of unusually large numbers of certain birds in Britain and Ireland usually means that a favoured food on their breeding grounds is in short supply. Attractive species such as the Redwing, Fieldfare, Brambling and Siskin may come to garden feeding areas.

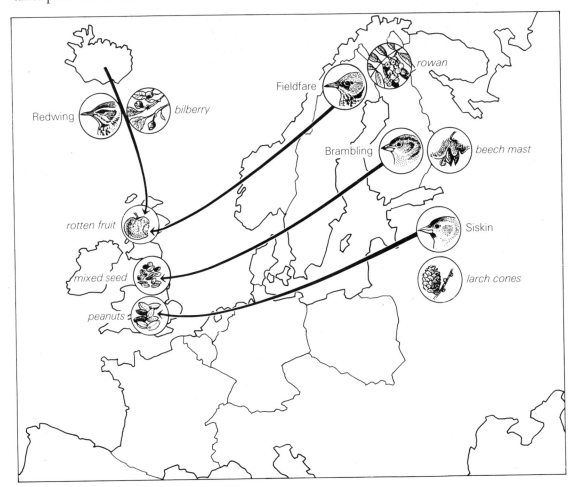

Brambling and is the result of an interaction between the bird numbers and their food supply. Fieldfares, for example, rely on rowan and other berries to see them through the winter, and take on a nomadic existence when the crop fails (see opposite).

The Siskin is another species which depends upon the seeds of a particular tree species, and its presence at garden bird tables is correspondingly irregular. Siskins normally breed in coniferous forests which they vacate in July and August when the cone seeds are exhausted, feeding instead in birches until migration.

In winter Siskins feed mostly on alder seeds, taking them at first from the cones but later from the ground below. Early each autumn a number of birds feed on seeds from the ground, these being dislodged by their conspecifics feeding above. They are probably younger birds as yet unable to open the green cones. As the cones ripen and the young birds gain in experience, they become increasingly adept at arboreal feeding and do not feed on the ground again until January, when the winter storms have scattered the ripened seeds to the ground. When these have been depleted in late winter the Siskins will resort to artificial food sources in gardens. Presumably in response to variations in the abundance of alder seeds they have appeared in varying numbers in gardens surveyed within the GBFS scheme; peak abundance occurs at 2–3 year intervals. Dr Ian Newton records the earliest date of this species eating fat in gardens as the mid 1960s, since when it has become more prevalent. One of the curious habits of this species is the tendency for the birds to concentrate their attention on peanuts contained within bright red plastic bags rather than in metal or wire feeders.

There is some evidence that Siskins are changing their habits in Britain. Until the 1970s there were few records of Siskins returning to winter a second time in an area they had frequented previously, a practice that is now more common. This may underlie the increased frequency with which Siskins are recorded at garden tables. One study suggests that the habit of feeding on nuts and fat in suburban gardens developed in Surrey and spread outwards as the technique was learned by young birds and conspecifics in the flock. It may well be that the increased tendency of humans to provide food on garden tables is encouraging the birds to return to the same place from year to year, thus allowing them to develop new habits. As noted earlier (p. 122), there is some evidence that Greenfinches are coming in to gardens for artificial food increasingly each year.

The numbers of birds actually appearing at a garden feeder are thus dependent on several factors. By and large, birds prefer to feed on natural foods, though some species such as Greenfinches are learning of the existence of an easy and reliable food source in gardens. Many garden species flock in winter and live a life regulated by the social hierarchies prevailing there, and those for whom such a life is toughest – notably the inexperienced juveniles – are most likely to leave to forage in gardens. But even the most experienced birds are likely to follow them into gardens when natural foods are scarce or when weather conditions are severe, and the foods they find there may determine, for many birds, whether they will survive the winter to breed the following spring. A small number of species such as Coal Tit and Marsh Tit have evolved a specialised food-hoarding behaviour which allows them to exploit the foods available while temporarily in surplus. Others defend distinct territories against their conspecifics or against rival flocks. Some of these points are, perhaps, complex in detail, but to know a little about them is to gain insight into the Clapham Junction of the bird table.

The Brambling is a delightful, if irregular, winter visitor to our gardens, coming mainly when local beech mast has been exhausted. Although it prefers to feed on a mixture of seeds from the ground, some individuals will first hover and then cling to the nut basket for peanuts.

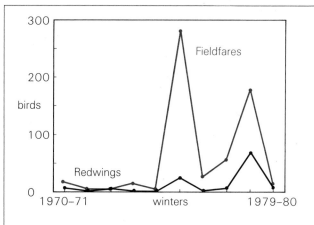

Fluctuating numbers

When the berry crop is good and survival of Fieldfares through the winter is consequently high, large numbers of the birds breed and produce many young. When such high populations of birds then encounter a resting year for the trees, in which relatively few berries are produced, the food supply is exhausted in mid or even early winter and the birds must move onwards in search of food. They move south and westwards until they reach the British Isles, settling first on the winter berries there, and then later, as these are exhausted, moving in to feed in gardens. Thus in some years large numbers of Fieldfares (right) and Redwings (left) are recorded at garden feeding areas, in other years very few indeed. Both species are most likely to be seen in gardens in January and February: by March spring subsong has resumed and the birds are beginning to show a certain amount of chasing and aggression prior to their return migration to the breeding grounds. The graph above shows annual sightings of Redwings and Fieldfares at GBFS sites between 1970 and 1980, showing the effect of irruption years.

Bramblings, another irruptive species from the northern forests, are most frequently seen in February and March. Like the Fieldfare, the Brambling will exploit rowan berries where the crop is good, and in Finland the local population may vary twentyfold according to the level of the rowan berry crop. In Britain, however, the main food of the Brambling is beech mast, and the bird therefore shares with the Chaffinch a tendency to stay outside gardens until late winter when the crop is exhausted. Bramblings leave Britain from early March onwards, with practically all birds gone by the end of April, and this is reflected in the attendance at bird tables.

8 Water: drinking and bathing

There have been a number of investigations into the food requirements of birds in the past, some of them detailed analyses of the preferences of individual species, but considerably less attention has been directed towards their drinking and bathing habits. All warm blooded creatures need water, but in many cases the amount necessary to support life has been reduced to an absolute minimum. Examples can be found among mammals as well as birds, and they are not necessarily those species which have had to adapt to desert or near-desert conditions. Two related mammals present contrasting examples of this. House mice are able to live and breed when confined with no access to free water, all their requirements being obtained from ingested grain with a water content of just 10 per cent, while rats must have drinking water at least once every 24 hours.

Among birds, too, certain species can endure long periods without free water. Budgerigars have been kept in good health for 150 days and Australian Zebra Finches for eighteen months on a diet of dry seed only. Metabolic water in these cases is the only water available. Water is conserved as much as possible by reducing its loss through the skin and when breathing. The faeces are brought into an extremely dry state. An experiment with a Budgerigar showed that with unlimited access to water the excreta can be 75–80 per cent water, while a bird deprived of water will reduce the percentage to 60. Certain species have also eliminated the necessity of having water for bathing by substituting dust-bathing for the more conventional method. Peafowl, partridges, pheasants and Quail rarely appear to bathe in water; House Sparrows are perhaps unique in bathing

In contrast to most other birds pigeons, such as this Woodpigeon, and certain game birds, are able to take in water continuously, using a sucking action. Once found, a drinking spot may be visited regularly each day.

133

indiscriminately in either dust or water – but then, House Sparrows appear to be able to adapt to almost any conditions, which is obviously one of the reasons why they are so successful as a species.

Varying needs for water

Clearly this variability in drinking and bathing habits merited further investigation, so birds making visits to the feeding area when water was also taken were recorded by the late H.G. Hurrell in his garden in South Brent, Devon. This was not a difficult task; food preferences were already being monitored so all that was needed was a further column on the recording sheet in which to indicate the visit to the bird bath, and by using a dot to record each visit a large number of visits could be accommodated in each column. Such records are, of course, inevitably a minimum score because it is obviously impossible to have the bird bath under constant surveillance from dawn to dusk over a long period. In this case recording took place during breakfast each morning but only spasmodically for the remainder of the day. Although this sounds rather casual it appears to work remarkably well. Bathing records were few but these were also noted on the back of the recording sheet.

Mud is essential to House Martins for nest building. They may find it in puddles or on the edges of ponds or streams; alternatively it can be provided in the garden in a washing-up bowl or old sink, which is very useful for the birds in times of drought, since if mud is unavailable and they cannot nest the House Martin population decreases.

In order to understand the results fully it is important to know something of the conditions in which the observations took place. The garden and the bird table are in an unusually isolated spot. There are no houses nearby and the nearest bird table is about 1 kilometre away. There is a 5 acre (2 hectare) wood beside the house, and a swimming pool and a lily pond about 100 metres away, but it is unusual to see birds using either of these for drinking or bathing. They appear to be instinctively aware of the dangers of deep or fast-flowing water, so that even in completely natural surroundings only certain safe access points are used at all regularly. A heap of twigs or debris caught up beside the river bank or a spit of sand at a bend in a stream may provide a safe place from which the water can be approached gradually, but if there are puddles in the lane or other small shallow pools of water these will almost certainly be preferred.

The influence of the weather

As might be expected, weather conditions have a marked influence on the drinking habits of birds, but when temperatures are near normal many of them appear to manage quite well on the fluid content of their food. During the four years from 1976 to 1980 the records show 53 weeks when either only one drink or none at all were noted. Against this there are 20 weeks with more than 50 records, and a glance at the weather conditions prevailing at the time of these periods of abnormal activity is all that is required to show the effects of a prolonged dry spell induced by either high temperatures or periods of hard frost. (Birds need extra water in hot weather for evaporative cooling, as part of their normal heat regulation.)

The weekly figures for the summer of 1976 (see below) show even more clearly the dramatic reduction in drinking which followed the change from hot dry weather to cooler, wet conditions, but they also indicate that at this time of year another factor has to be taken into account: the number of species recorded is also considerably reduced, since by October many of them are well on their way to their winter quarters.

It should not be thought, however, that a prolonged drought is necessary to boost the popularity of the bird bath. During the 1976 drought the highest weekly count was 150 visits, but this was easily exceeded in 1978 when an exceptionally hot but short spell in July produced a total of 200 visits. In the week preceding this there had been 22 and in the week which followed it only a single visit was recorded; the weather in July 1978 was certainly changeable.

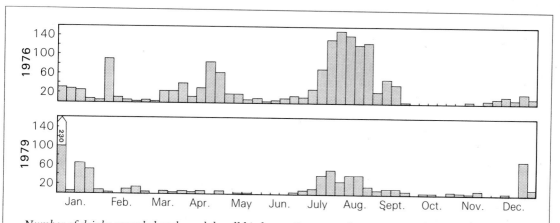

Number of drinks recorded each week by all birds at a Devon garden water tray during 1976 and 1979.

The effects of drought

The exceptionally dry summer of 1976 provides an excellent example of this, showing as it does the marked increase in visits to the bird bath as the weeks passed and the natural sources vanished. The monthly figures show a dramatic increase as the drought intensified; in May there were 54, in June 34, but in July there were 399 visits, and as the sun beat down on a parched and arid countryside throughout August the total reached an unprecedented 458. Predictions about the terrible after-effects of the drought were rife, but unjustified. Torrential rains in September quickly restored the vegetation and England was once more a 'green and pleasant land' – and the number of visits to the bird bath fell to 34; in October it was a mere two.

While the number of visits in hot weather can be impressive, cold spells can be equally noteworthy. Indeed, they may well be far more dramatic, since during hot spells alternative supplies dry up gradually, but in times of severe frost all these natural supplies are liable to dry up, or freeze up, simultaneously. One day there are ample supplies, the next day there are none. During the first week in January 1979 much of Britain experienced a spell of arctic weather with heavy snowfall followed by sub-zero temperatures for several successive days, and in that week a record total of 230 birds drinking at the bird bath was recorded. Then came the sudden thaw, and in the following week there were just three visits (p. 135).

There is always a tendency for birds to drink more at the bird bath in winter than in summer. In the summer months most birds remain in their breeding territories, and the area in the immediate vicinity of drinking facilities provided in the garden can only hold a limited number of these. In winter territorial rivalry is considerably less acute, and if liberal quantities of food are provided birds from a wide area around the garden will be attracted, though the numerical

House Sparrows bathe in water in gardens all year round — it is important for keeping their feathers in good condition. Their recent scarcity in some rural areas has been attributed to increased efficiency in farming, involving the drainage of many farm ponds.

strength of the different species will be found to vary considerably. Great Tits, Blue Tits, Coal Tits and Greenfinches will arrive in considerable numbers and, having fed, may need to drink or bathe; Nuthatches, Great Spotted Woodpeckers and Marsh Tits, on the other hand, seem to take up territories very early in the autumn, and these territories are often maintained throughout the year so that it is quite unusual to see more than two Nuthatches or a pair of Great Spotted Woodpeckers at the drinking place at any one time.

Robins are reputed to be fairly aggressive but their territorial instincts are relaxed in winter if times are hard and several will often be found around the area where food and water are still available. There will be minor skirmishes, which become more noticeable at the end of the winter or in very early spring, but as a rule they are not serious and most of the contestants appear to go away satisfied. Blackbirds, too: there is only room for a single Blackbird on the average bird table but if windfall apples are scattered around the lawn as many as a dozen may be present. All these factors need to be taken into consideration when attempting to assess the importance of water to the various species; three observed visits to the water by Nuthatches or Redpolls may indicate a far greater need for water by these species than a dozen visits by Blue Tits or Starlings.

A study of birds' drinking and bathing habits

The early results from this local enquiry suggested that it might be interesting to widen its scope, and it was suggested to the Devon Bird Watching and Preservation Society that they might adopt the project. Initially quite a modest scheme was envisaged, but in fact it developed into a massive undertaking with the participants submitting not far short of 200,000 observations in three separate surveys. The first of these was a pilot survey, designed to see what support might be expected and to suggest the avenues which might profitably be explored. This took place in March, April and May 1975, and was so successful that it was followed almost immediately by a full scale, six-month survey from October 1975 to March 1976.

Enthusiasm for the project was maintained, and as it seemed a pity to have a full survey for only half of the year, another was organised for April to September 1977 to complete the picture, but with a gap of one year between the two six-month periods. The response was quite amazing, showing clearly the popularity of any form of garden birdwatching which can be undertaken by observers whose activities are limited, for a variety of reasons, to what can be seen from the windows of the house. The winter survey alone produced 100,000 observations from 85 people, and the summer one 72,000 from 50 participants. In addition there were several thousand records from the pilot survey – and all from a single county which is not particularly heavily populated.

The objectives of the project were:

1   To study the relative importance of drinking and bathing to birds using garden bird baths.

2   To find out if weather conditions have any marked effect on the birds' drinking and bathing habits.

3   To discover which birds do not appear to use such facilities, or which use them only for drinking or only for bathing.

The tables below, summarising the results, show at a glance that the number of drinks far exceeds the number of bathes. It is also clear that the numbers, particularly those referring to drinking, fluctuate widely. In winter the highest number of drinks occurred in January (see p. 136), when the temperatures are usually at their lowest, often

---

'Top ten' drinking and bathing species

(Based on a survey by the Devon Bird Watching and Preservation Society)

TOWN AND SUBURBAN GARDENS

	1978 summer survey	Average no. per observer	1976/77 winter survey	Average no. per observer
Frequency of drinking				
House Sparrow	1	627	1	399
Starling	2	276	2	192
Greenfinch	3	141	4	60
Blackbird	4	116	3	89
Blue Tit	5=	49	6	38
Collared Dove	5=	49	7	30
Chaffinch	7	48	5	39
Dunnock	8	25	10	15
Robin	9	15	8	27
Song Thrush	10	11	9	21
Frequency of bathing				
Starling	1	208	1	136
House Sparrow	2	136	2	80
Blackbird	3	67	3	51
Blue Tit	4	20	4	24
Robin	5	13	5	19
Dunnock	6	8.8	9	3.2
Song Thrush	7	7.7	6	10.5
Great Tit	8	5	7	4.2
Chaffinch	9	3.8	(11=)	(2.3)
Coal Tit	10	1.7	(11=)	(2.3)
Greenfinch	(11)	(1.4)	10	2.7
Wren	(12)	(1.3)	8	4

with freezing conditions. The summer figures build up to peak numbers during the hottest months, July and August.

The number of species recorded in the various gardens during these surveys showed considerable variation according to the location of the garden. One garden on the outskirts of Paignton in Devon recorded no less than 25 different species during the first six-month period, and precisely twice this number were noted when the records of all the observers were combined for the same period. The summer survey produced slightly fewer (43 species), probably, again, since many of our summer visitors might be expected to return directly to their breeding territories and not all of them habitually breed in and around gardens.

Much depends on the situation of the garden and the type of vegetation in the immediate vicinity. Turtle Dove, Whitethroat, Garden Warbler, Blackcap, Chiffchaff, Willow Warbler and Spotted

VILLAGE AND COUNTRY GARDENS

	1978 summer survey	Average no. per observer	1976/77 winter survey	Average no. per observer
Frequency of drinking				
House Sparrow	1	304	1	234
Starling	2	136	2	199
Blackbird	3	94	4	50
Chaffinch	4	79	5	40
Blue Tit	5	38	3	109
Collared Dove	6	32	(13)	(5)
Greenfinch	7	21	6	34
Robin	8	15	9	16
Great Tit	9	12	7	22
Woodpigeon	10	10	(15)	(2.5)
Dunnock	(11)	(7)	10	9
Coal Tit	(12)	(5)	8	18
Frequency of bathing				
Starling	1	136	1	71
House Sparrow	2	61	4	31
Blackbird	3	46	3	38
Blue Tit	4	17	2	40
Chaffinch	5	13	8	5
Robin	6	11	5	15
Dunnock	7	5	9	3
Song Thrush	8	4	6	8
Great Tit	9	3	7	7
Pied Wagtail	10	2.7	(13)	(0.8)
Greenfinch	(11)	(1.9)	(15)	(0.5)
Wren	(17)	(1.3)	10	2

Note: Figures are bracketed when the species is out of the 'top ten'

Nature's safeguard

Most tree seeds are only scattered by the wind in dry weather; in the case of the Scots pine, for example, the cones remain tightly closed during damp weather so that the seed is not available to the majority of birds. The opening and closing of the cones according to the humidity of the atmosphere is nature's way of ensuring that the seed is carried by the wind for a considerable distance, for if this seed were damp it would fall heavily immediately around the parent tree. It also means that the seed itself has a very low water content when it is available to the birds, so if there are coniferous trees around the garden the number of finch species (right, a Crossbill) visiting the bird bath during April and May, when the seed is ripe, will increase.

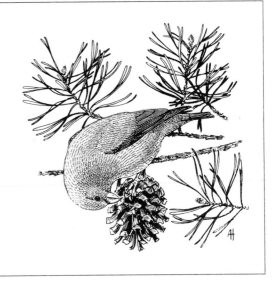

Flycatcher are the summer migrants most often appearing at the bird bath; rarely a surprise Redstart or Nightingale. Birds feeding on tree seeds are regular visitors to any available water supply because of the low moisture content of this food. In the garden most of the food which the birds take will be wet or dry according to the weather, and if it is wet much of their water requirement will be taken up almost inadvertently, so that no extra drinking may be necessary.

The drinking habits of different species

Since our most familiar garden birds tend to be the resident species – tits, finches, thrushes and Starlings – it is not surprising that the species appearing in the lists of visitors to the bird bath in both winter and summer are somewhat similar. It is also clear that in all cases it is the species which are attracted into the garden in order to feed on the artificial foods provided which are most likely to avail themselves of the equally 'artificial' water supply. Other species drink, but they are unlikely to visit the garden for that purpose alone except in conditions of extreme drought or hard frost. For the remainder of the time they will make do with streams, puddles, dew or raindrops sipped from the foliage around them.

House Sparrows easily head the lists in both summer and winter, followed by Starling, Greenfinch, Blackbird, Blue Tit, Collared Dove, Chaffinch, Dunnock, Robin and Song Thrush. There are minor differences in the positions of these when the winter and summer lists are compared, but the 'top ten' species are similar in both instances. It is noticeable that no summer migrant has managed to displace a resident species on the summer list, but when the records received by the Devon Bird Watching and Preservation Society were divided into rural and urban/suburban sites, the Collared Dove and Song Thrush, which had appeared on the urban list, were displaced in rural gardens by Coal Tit and Great Tit.

Several observers commented on the reluctance of the Wren to make use of the bird bath for either drinking or bathing, and in a few gardens the three common tits, the Dunnock, the Goldcrest, the Magpie, the Jackdaw and even the Chaffinch and Greenfinch were recorded as infrequent visitors, but as a number of these appear in the 'top ten' lists for most gardens these observations were obviously affected by local conditions – probably by an alternative source nearby. One interesting observation was that although there was not a single instance of a Long-tailed Tit visiting the bird bath during the summer, in winter there were 69 records, suggesting that the species' winter diet has a much lower water content than its summer fare.

It is suggested that the water requirement of female birds may increase immediately before the eggs are laid, a theory put forward by Dr Leonard Hurrell who noted this phenomenon during his work with breeding birds of prey in captivity. While this sounds quite probable and, if substantiated, would almost certainly apply to other

When sipping water, the Crossbill looks ungainly with its crossed mandibles, which are an adaptation for extracting seeds from cones. It breeds in the conifer forests of northern Europe and erupts in certain summers, such as 1963, when large numbers were reported in gardens.

species as well as predators, it will be difficult to prove except under the controlled conditions provided by an aviary.

Most birds when drinking scoop up a beakful of water, raise the head and allow the water to trickle down the throat, often repeating the process several times. All pigeons and doves, however, drink by sucking up a continuous draught of water. This is commented on by Derek Goodwin in his book *Pigeons and Doves of the World*, where he says 'immediately after [drinking] the bird lifts its head and slightly expands its gape, presumably taking a deep breath just as we do after drinking deeply.' Crows have a habit of dunking large food items in water before eating them, but the object is probably to soften the food rather than to take in water.

Bathing for cleanliness and protection

While drinking is a necessity in order to support life, bathing is an optional activity. Not all species of birds bathe in water. Game birds – pheasants, partridges and Quail – bathe in dust, and in certain respects this may serve the same purpose as the more conventional method. Swifts, Swallows and martins rarely bathe in the normal manner adopted by perching birds. Swifts find it extremely difficult to rise from a flat surface even when dry; when they were

The dry, dusty soil of a regularly tilled vegetable patch or herbaceous border will be used by House Sparrows for dust bathing, and in country districts Pheasants (below) may join in. Vigorous scratching and shuffling of the wings, with body feathers raised, ensures that dust filters through the full plumage.

Birds wet their plumage so that subsequent preening or oiling, or both, may be done more efficiently. This Blackbird shows the typical bathing action, moving its head, wings and to a lesser extent its tail, and ruffling its body feathers.

thoroughly soaked they would almost certainly find it impossible. However, one Devon watcher saw a Swallow fly repeatedly through the spray thrown up by bathing Starlings, and Sand Martins have been recorded using dew-soaked grass in which to perform their ablutions. It must be remembered, however, that we know little about what these aerial birds do for much of their lives. We do know that Swifts sleep on the wing and that they can mate while in flight so it is quite possible that a heavy downpour might give them the opportunity to take at least a sketchy bath. Further summer visitors including Blackcap and Willow Warbler bathe effectively by brushing their plumage through rain-soaked foliage.

Most garden birds bathe occasionally, often in cold, wet weather when conditions appear to us to be quite unsuitable, so there must be a good reason behind this. Cleanliness suggests itself; one has only to see the difference between a city-born House Sparrow and its country cousin to appreciate that dust and grime accumulates on a bird's plumage just as it does on everything else, and an occasional bath may help to remove some of it. Bathing may help, too, in controlling external parasites to which the bird plays unwilling host, and it is certainly true that those species having the least opportunity to bathe – the hirundines and Swift – are those most likely to be heavily infested with ticks, lice, mites and other unwelcome

143

The design of the feather

A feather is a beautifully designed object. From the shaft or quill the barbs run in parallel rows, those nearest the tip being slightly shorter than those lower down. Along the edges of these barbs are further branches, almost invisible to the naked eye, called barbules, and along the edge facing the tip of the feather each barbule carries a row of minute hooks which engage in the scroll-like barbules on the opposite side of the neighbouring barbule. (Man has recently adapted this principle to his own benefit with the invention of Velcro.) If we take a feather and rub it from the tip towards the quill, the hooks are disengaged, the feather immediately becomes untidy and gaps appear along the shaft; but if we stroke in the opposite direction, towards the tip, the hooks re-engage and the feather is restored. This is exactly what happens when the bird preens, and the hooks and scrolls produce a web so strong that little air or water can penetrate.

guests. Either reason might give the birds cause to bathe; neither would explain why they so often choose to bathe late in the evening or when the weather is particularly inclement.

Perhaps the third reason – the birds' need to ensure that their plumage is always maintained in perfect condition – is the most important of all.

A healthy, full grown bird may appear to be completely covered with feathers, but in fact it will have extensive bare areas which are covered by rows of feathers on either side. It is essential therefore that every feather is in exactly the right position, particularly on cold nights, to ensure that all these areas are completely covered. The body feathers trap a layer of warm air between feathers and body; a bird which is sick or cold will raise its feathers to increase the amount of air so trapped, and a sleeping bird will often appear to be 'fluffed up' for the same reason.

Most birds preen at intervals during the day, rearranging a feather here and a feather there, but the preening which follows a good soaking in the bird bath is a much more meticulous affair, every feather receiving the bird's undivided attention. If this thorough preening takes place when the weather is particularly foul, or late in the evening when the temperature has fallen below zero, it seems reasonable to suggest that this is the bird's way of preparing for the difficult conditions which it has foreseen.

Birds seldom appear to get very wet even during a heavy rainstorm because their carefully preened plumage forms an almost completely waterproof barrier, but when taking a bath the feathers are raised, allowing the water to penetrate to the skin, and vigorous shaking ensures that even the back is soaked. Perhaps the most striking example of the effectiveness of a feathered covering is given by the Dipper, which spends much of its life in the water, even walking along the bed of a fast flowing stream, completely submerged, when searching for the aquatic larvae on which it feeds. H.G. Hurrell, during a study of this species in South Devon, found that it was 'customary for the Dipper to have a deliberate and thorough bathe before going to roost'. Obviously in this case cleanliness can be discounted as a motive, but the need to maintain a completely waterproof covering is even greater, and a thorough bathe is the most effective way of achieving this.

There were a number of comments in the Devon surveys on the bathing behaviour of various species. Song Thrushes and Blackbirds were frequently reported as visiting the bird bath for a quick dip after a spell of incubation. Dunnocks, unobtrusive and retiring birds at the best of times, appeared to be timid bathers, entering the water

Dippers are birds of fast-flowing streams where they feed in and under the water. Although they are relatives of such 'normal' terrestrial species as Robins and Blackbirds their lives are very aquatic. They are able to swim under water with their wings acting as oars, and they use their strong feet to grasp the stream bottom.

to flick a few drops over their feathers then returning to the edge of the bath to preen before repeating the process, often several times. There were no records of nocturnal birds either drinking or bathing in gardens, but a number of ringed owls of various species have been 'found drowned' in water butts and swimming pools, so the omission may have been due to the inability of the observers to see in the dark! One observation made by H. G. Hurrell, while otter watching beside the River Plym many years ago, must be unique: 'At dusk a Nightjar flew out over the middle of the river where it hovered momentarily about a metre above the water before plunging right under. It then rose quickly, shaking the water from its feathers as it flew off.' The Nightjar can hardly be called a 'garden bird', but it is a most relevant story.

Some species appear to tolerate and even to enjoy a communal bath, and there is a suggestion that an imitative element creeps in where the flocking species – Long-tailed and Blue Tits, Starlings,

In social species, such as Starlings, communal bathing is common and fun to watch. One bird's activity triggers off others, and the water begins to fly. The birds' aim is to stand in the water and wet their plumage evenly, without actually soaking it, as a preliminary to preening.

Above: The Siskin (left) and Greenfinch (right) are seed-eating finches that make regular visits to drink at the garden pool. When appearing together they are noticeably intolerant, posturing aggressively, each species showing its bold yellow wing markings and side tail flashes.

House Sparrows and Greenfinches – are concerned, so that the sight of one bird bathing may trigger off the desire in others to join in. The less sociable birds, such as Pied Wagtails, Robins, Blackbirds and thrushes, on the other hand, will often aggressively defend their right to bathe alone.

Much can be learned from a study such as that carried out by the Devon Bird Watching and Preservation Society and we are grateful to them for permission to publish material resulting from their surveys. The information obtained in this way is the more valuable since it concerns birds living as the participants in the GBFS believe they should live – free to come and go as they please, free to take advantage of the early morning dew for a drink or a dip or to make use of the bird bath if they wish. It is probably impossible to assess the physical effects of drinking except under controlled conditions in the cage or aviary, and most of the experiments which have been undertaken to date have been done in this way. Such things are for the laboratory scientist; for the garden bird enthusiast it is sufficient to provide the bird bath, see that it is always full and let the birds provide the data.

147

9 Cold weather

Somewhat surprisingly, if October is mild many more birds of a species will be seen feeding at bird tables than is the case if the month is cold. Of the top 30 most frequently recorded species in the GBFS 22 species are more numerous in suburban (23 species in rural) gardens in mild Octobers. Presumably this is because many juveniles can survive if the weather is mild and are moving around seeking a place in which to establish themselves for the winter. In November the same effect is apparent, but to a less marked extent: 18 of the top 30 species are more prevalent in suburban gardens, 16 species in rural gardens, if November is mild. As the winter deepens even fewer birds show this pattern, and by December less than half the species respond in this way, probably because more of the juveniles have died or more of the adults have moved out of the country. Birds that behave in this way include Blue and Great Tits, Dunnock, Pied Wagtail, Wren and Magpie.

Other species come into gardens in large numbers only if the weather is cold and are less numerous there in warm weather. Examples include several of the thrushes – Robin, Blackbird, Song Thrush and Mistle Thrush – as well as Starling, Black-headed Gull, Jackdaw, Great Spotted Woodpecker, and even (in the case of rural gardens) the House Sparrow. For these species there are many alternative natural foods in early winter, giving the birds the opportunity to respond to an unusually cold month without resorting to artificial foods. Later in the winter, however, these additional food sources are not available and the birds must resort to artificial foods if they are to survive.

Throughout the year the Blackbird is a familiar bird in gardens, where many of the estimated breeding population of 7 million pairs in Britain and Ireland are to be found. Hard weather seems to affect it much less than other vulnerable species like the Song Thrush, Wren and Pied Wagtail. However, detailed studies have shown that its survival through periods of frost depends on its ability to build up very substantial reserves of fat by industrious feeding through the short winter days.

149

Equally interesting are those species that do not respond at all to the prevailing temperature as far as exploiting bird table foods is concerned. Chaffinch, Greenfinch, Coal Tit and Collared Dove are examples among the top twenty, plus three irruptive species, the Redwing, Fieldfare and Brambling, and from the next ten most frequent species two crows, the Rook and Carrion Crow. These are of course all species that have widespread natural food supplies (see Chapter 7): the finches of mast and weed seeds, the Coal Tit of food hoarded in autumn, the Collared Dove of farmyard grain, etc., so they are perhaps less sensitive to the impact of cold weather.

Among the smallest birds resident in Britain the Goldcrest feeds almost continuously throughout the day in midwinter; Long-tailed Tits spend 90–95 per cent of their time feeding, Coal Tits about 90 per cent, Blue Tits 85 per cent and Great Tits 75 per cent. The amount of time spent feeding is thus related to the body size of the bird. Under cold conditions, therefore, the smaller species are under some pressure to obtain enough food. One way to increase the feeding time available is to start earlier and remain later, and this is indeed what birds seem to do in the winter. In one study, Blue Tits feeding at a bird table were found to arrive an average of 17 minutes before sunrise in January but only 7 minutes before sunrise in March. For Great Tits the corresponding figures are 10 and 5 minutes respectively. Departure from the bird table was similarly delayed in January, Blue Tits leaving 24 minutes after sunset against 17 minutes in March, and Great Tits staying on for 8 minutes in January but only 4 minutes in March.

Feeding rhythms and fat reserves

The effect of weather on the daily feeding rhythm of birds has been poorly studied in Britain, since few observers have the time to monitor the rate at which birds feed throughout the day. However, it is known from work in the United States that birds put on more weight during the hours they spend most time feeding and are

During the course of an average winter's day an adult Great Tit weighing 20 g needs to consume 6.8 g of mixed seeds, about one-third of its body weight, in order to satisfy its complete energy requirements.

lighter during periods when they do not feed intensively. This is not an altogether surprising finding. Looking at the weights of birds in relation to time of day thus tells us something about how intensively the birds have been feeding recently (see below).

Some idea of the demands placed on urban Blackbirds by winter conditions can be gained by comparing weights in two months: in April body weights are in the range 90–95 g, but in January they are of the order 115–120 g. Most of the difference is fat, the main fuel used for immediate metabolism by birds, but a proportion of it may be food carried into the roosts by Blackbirds feeding right up to the last possible moment. In the case of granivorous birds with crops, many fly to the roost with their crops filled with seeds gathered in during the last available time for feeding.

How much fat can a bird carry without it interfering with its normal activities? Humans are familiar with the idea of strength being related to size; we know that it is easier for a 14 stone man to lift a heavy bag than for a man of 9 stone to do so, even if both men are equally fit. The same principle applies to birds: it has been found that big birds can carry more fat than small birds. Of course, being bigger the larger species need more fat, but their needs do not increase in proportion to their size: a 20 g bird needs only 59 per cent

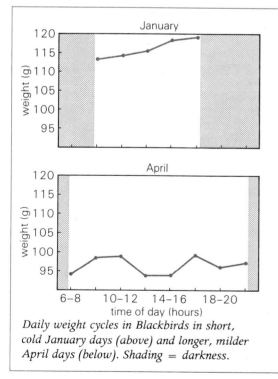

Daily weight cycles in Blackbirds in short, cold January days (above) and longer, milder April days (below). Shading = darkness.

Winter and summer feeding patterns

In a study of Blackbirds near London, carried out in midwinter and spring by Dr Leo Batten, it was found that during the colder period the birds, having spent the night in the shelter of the roost but still in rather cool conditions, would leave the roost with fat reserves heavily depleted and feed intensively throughout the day. Thus life in winter for a Blackbird consists of intensive feeding through a short day and a build-up of fat reserves, followed by nights in which these reserves are depleted again. In contrast, there was found to be a clear daily rhythm of feeding implicit in the April weights. The birds left the roost hungry in the early morning and fed intensively for the first two to four hours until they had assuaged their hunger. Feeding activity in late morning and early afternoon was less intensive and the weight of the birds gradually declined until 6 p.m. or so, when a burst of evening feeding took place as they built up some fat reserves to see them through the night again.

The effect of cold on energy needs

At one roost in February on two occasions only eight days apart Blackbird energy requirements varied from 16.4 Kcal (the unit in which energy is measured) on a night when the average temperature was 5.5 °C to 23.7 Kcal on a night with a mean temperature of − 2.8 °C. Following their experience of the colder night the Blackbirds went to roost the following evening carrying an extra 8.5 g of weight. Thus within a single month the difference in temperature resulted in a nearly 50 per cent difference in energy requirement, subsequently reflected in the birds' body weight adjustment.

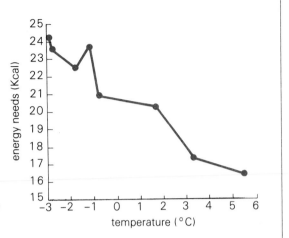

as much fat as a 10 g bird, to allow them both the same amount of metabolic activity. One consequence of this is that larger birds can live longer in any given set of environmental conditions. They can therefore search longer to find new food sources than small birds can. This is undoubtedly one of the key reasons why smaller birds are more desperate for food in cold conditions, and why it is the smaller species that flock more readily into the garden.

It has been shown that the survival rate of Blue Tits during winter is closely related to the temperatures they experience in early winter: if the temperature is mild then, the rest of the winter is usually (but not always) also mild and the birds survive well to breed again the following spring. But if it is cold in November fewer Blue Tits survive, and the breeding population the following spring is depressed. It seems likely, though no one has yet proven it, that juvenile birds are particularly at risk in early winter, for this will probably be their first experience of major environmental stress since becoming independent of their parents. In England and Wales the average monthly temperature decreases from about 16 °C in July to under 4 °C in January and February, but more than half of this decrease occurs between September and November. There is thus a very short period in which young birds must adapt to the rigours of winter.

What are the problems posed for birds by low temperatures? In cold weather they lose heat more rapidly than in warm weather. They must therefore increase their rate of heat production, and this means they need more food to fuel their metabolism. Not only must the birds find additional food to cope with low temperatures by day, they must also accumulate a larger reserve of fat to meet their

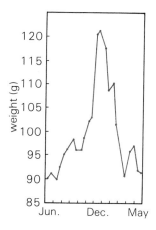

Mean weights of male Blackbirds in different months of the year.

metabolic costs in the night. Ability to increase body weight to carry the extra metabolic reserves needed to see it through cold nights is an important part of a bird's adaptive response to the winter season.

In the figure on the left you can see weight variation recorded at a Blackbird roost over several winters. One can hardly conceive of a human undergoing a weight cycle from 9 stone to 12 stone in the course of each year, yet this is what the Blackbirds do relative to their weight. That is, in midwinter a male Blackbird is carrying an additional one-third of its summer body weight by way of reserves. Part of this is necessitated by the longer nights of midwinter: in summer the bird has only about eight hours during which it will not be able to feed and has to rely upon stored reserves, while in winter it has perhaps twice this period of obligatory roosting. In addition, the lower temperatures of midwinter necessitate a higher metabolism, so whatever reserves the bird does have are being consumed at a faster rate.

Roosting in cold weather

During periods of cold weather birds have to spend the day feeding and must fly to the food source, irrespective of the local weather. At night, however, they can save energy by roosting in the most sheltered spots available. In Dr Leo Batten's study in the late 1960s of Blackbirds in London, the roost being studied was located in a blackthorn and hawthorn thicket sheltered on two sides by houses. This roost afforded its occupants considerable reduction in exposure to windy conditions: inside the roost the average wind speed was about 30 cm per second (approximately 0.7 mph) while outside the roost the wind averaged 104 cm per second (approximately 2.3 mph). Such a reduction in wind speed is vitally important because of the 'wind chill' effect (see below). Blackbirds temporarily

Insulation

For birds (as humans), sitting quietly in absolutely still air results in the layer of air immediately above the body surface gradually becoming warmed up, so that heat is carried away from the body relatively slowly. If a wind is blowing over the bird this layer of warm air is rapidly dissipated, and the bird loses heat at a faster rate. Such heat losses require greater metabolism of fat reserves during the night and consequently the bird must find even greater amounts of food during the day time.

hold captive inside the roosts metabolised only 2.35 g of fat, while others held in cages outside the roost lost 3.41 g. Thus the shelter afforded by the roost enabled the Blackbirds to get by with 31 per cent less fat on an average night. Even on the calmest of winter nights the difference was 26 per cent, and on the windiest nights the saving was 55 per cent. Moreover, within the roost the birds used only the more sheltered bushes.

Which is more important to the birds, the length of time they have to spend in the roost or the temperature they experience there? It seems that the answer depends on the time of year: in October Blackbirds caught on different nights varied in weight according to whether it was a cold or a warm night and whether it was early or late in the month (and therefore with different night lengths); the latter was found to be twice as important as the former. Throughout the winter, however, temperature became steadily more important, so that by February the temperature experienced by the birds was almost the only thing of importance to them. This of course reflects also the general change in winter climate in the British Isles, for it is well known that a cold night in February is more likely to produce snowfall, persistent frost and other severe weather than are the equivalent conditions in October and November. By March night lengths have begun to be more important once more, and temperature is less severe a regulator of the bird's food requirements. This can be seen in the seasonal pattern of weight variation for, in a mild winter, March weights have fallen to almost summer levels, while in a colder winter these weights have fallen but not to quite the same extent.

Thinking ahead

Yellowhammers coming to roost each evening have been shown to be able to predict how much food they will normally need for the time of year and store fat to match. That is, when overnight temperatures were likely to be low the birds being studied arrived at the roost with more fat than when temperatures were likely to be high. This would not be surprising if the birds were responding to the temperatures they were currently experiencing, but this was not the case. The birds were accumulating reserves to see them through the expected temperatures, not the actual temperatures.

If Yellowhammers are able to predict their likely food requirements in this way they ought also to have evolved behaviour allowing them to alter their food-seeking habits – for example, by turning to garden feeding stations – when their normal behaviour is proving inadequate to supply them with food at the rate they anticipate they will need. Normally Yellowhammers carry just over a day's fat

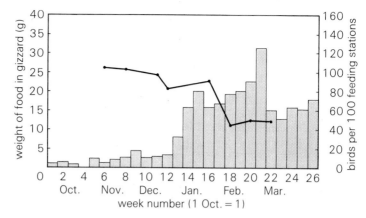

Yellowhammers feed intensively shortly before roosting to get food for their overnight energy needs. As food gets scarcer in late winter (line) more birds resort to garden feeders (bars). (Food data after Evans, 1968, J. Anim. Ecol. 38: 418.)

reserves, so they have this margin of warning if their main winter food – spilt grain on farmland – is running short. The figure above plots the average food (not fat) reserves carried by Yellowhammers into their woodland roost against the percentage of GBFS stations recording Yellowhammers throughout Britain. There is obviously a good relationship between the two, showing that Yellowhammers are leaving their natural farmland environment and moving to feed in gardens when they have trouble finding enough food.

How do the birds know about the existence of feeding stations in gardens when they don't normally go there? Yellowhammers roost in shrubs, thickets and small trees, often with other small song birds more common in gardens, such as Blackbirds and Chaffinches. It

Follow my leader

One of the most fascinating explanations advanced as to why roosts form at all has been the idea that they might serve as 'information centres' for the birds assembling in them. A bird which has experienced difficulty in obtaining enough food to satisfy its needs the previous day will not know in what direction it should leave the roost the following morning, since it does not know where the best food sources are. On the other hand, those birds that had a satisfactory food source the previous day will leave the roost fairly promptly, to get maximum feeding time in during the short winter day. One ploy for the birds that have failed to find adequate food the previous day would be to follow those well-fed birds and share in their food source. Left: Yellowhammers.

seems likely that the Yellowhammers follow the other birds to the feeding stations (see p. 155), and this behaviour must have evolved because those birds that became more sociable when hungry arrived at the new food sources and so survived better: the habit therefore spread. This type of learning must underlie some of the seasonal increases in the attendance of birds at garden feeding stations.

Taking the winter sun . . .

We know surprisingly little about the effect of winter sun on birds in the British Isles, but the behaviour of White-crowned Sparrows in the United States has been shown to alter with the extent of winter sun. On cold and cloudy days these sparrows feed intensively throughout the day, but on warm sunny days the amount of feeding is reduced during the middle of the day. Also, the birds consume less food during sunny than cloudy mornings, even when temperatures are very similar. This indicates that the birds need less food when the sun is shining.

At first sight this is a peculiar finding, but it has a simple explanation. When the sun is shining the surface layer of the feathers is heated, thus reducing the temperature gradient between the skin of the bird and the ambient temperature: less heat therefore flows from the bird and a lower metabolism (and therefore less food) is needed. This has been shown experimentally by scientists who dyed the white feathers of Zebra Finches black and exposed the birds to artificial sunlight. The dyed birds needed 25 per cent less food than their white counterparts. Presumably the experimental birds had to work harder for their living after the next moult when they recovered their white feathers once more!

. . . and following the sun

An alternative to coping with low temperatures is to migrate to warmer regions. Everyone is familiar with the idea of Swallows and other summer visitors leaving Britain for the winter. Less well known is the fact that some of our 'resident' birds migrate within Britain. Our island is not uniform in climate, Scotland being colder than the south-west, for example. Hence some birds might benefit by moving out for the winter. Those that don't but try to live through the winter in their usual residence pay for the benefit of being in occupation of territories so early in the following year by experiencing heavier mortality during the winter. Wrens in the coldest parts of Britain during the severe winter of 1978/79 suffered in this way.

One species that moves about like this is the Reed Bunting. The figure opposite shows how Reed Buntings in Britain move between

The Reed Bunting (above) is one of several species, such as the Great Spotted Woodpecker, Magpie, Siskin and Long-tailed Tit, now learning to visit gardens and take advantage of people's generosity. First appearing in suburban gardens at the onset of cold weather, they may then remain throughout the winter. The maps (right) show the long-distance movements of male and female Reed Buntings between breeding and wintering grounds in Britain, showing the greater tendency of females to move towards the warmer south and south-west for the winter.

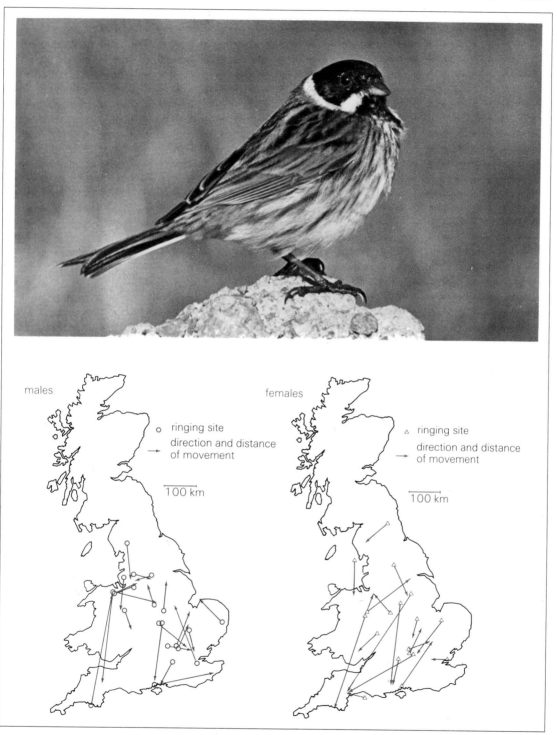

winter and summer quarters and vice versa. They move in a southerly direction or towards coastal regions for the winter and return in spring, and the female Reed Buntings move rather longer distances than the males. Dr Robert Prys-Jones, who has researched this species at the Edward Grey Institute in Oxford, estimated that only about 30 per cent of males but about 60 per cent of females move at least 5 km between winter and summer sites. Part of this difference between the sexes is related to differences in body size, as noted elsewhere for Great Tits (p. 125). Male Reed Buntings average 7 per cent larger than females and are dominant over the latter at food sources. Consequently female Reed Buntings migrate more (despite the risks involved in doing so) because they can survive better in milder areas. Of course, if they can avoid the risk of migrating they do so, and in milder winters rather more females remain on the breeding grounds than in colder winters. At Attenborough Gravel Pits, near Nottingham, the ratios of males to females were found to decrease from 3:1 in a cold winter towards 1:1 in a warm winter, and at Rye Meads, Hertfordshire, ratios were from 2.4:1 in cold winters to about 1.3:1 in warm ones. For resident species the ratio varies little from year to year.

The effect of cold winters on birds

What seems to matter most to birds is not icy conditions but *access* to food. Frozen ground is an effective stopper to such access (as also is snow), and the birds are forced to areas where food continues to be accessible, notably garden bird tables, around and inside open barns and animal sheds on farms, and along the edges of running water where the constant flow keeps water temperatures above freezing, the adjacent ground soft, and some invertebrate food constantly available. The winter of 1962/63 was excessively severe, with the ground frozen for many days on end without a thaw, and bird mortality was high. In 1978/79 similar conditions prevailed, but they were broken fairly frequently by short thaws which allowed the birds to stock up on food and water. In the milder winter of 1977/78, on the other hand, there were few unusual problems to be faced by the birds.

This sensitivity to frost is more pronounced for some species than for others. Birds taking invertebrate foods such as earthworms or snails are much more affected than seed-eating species. Even a short frost may deprive the invertebrate feeders of their usual fare and force them into gardens in search of food. Among these species are Black-headed Gulls, Snipe and Woodcock.

It is also significant that the invertebrate eaters are among those species most prone to movement in hard weather.

Thrushes on the move

During the severe cold and blizzards of December 1981 and January 1982, many thrushes moved out of Britain in search of milder conditions elsewhere. Ringing recoveries plotted on the map show that many moved to Ireland where the weather was severe only for a few days in mid-January, but a few moved southwards to France which remained less severe throughout. In normal winters such overseas recoveries are infrequent. The circles indicate the area where the birds were ringed, and the arrows the direction and distance of movement.

The movement of Song Thrushes is recorded above; other thrushes are well known for their movements out of Britain into the milder climate of Ireland during cold spells in Britain. Lapwings rarely appear at garden feeding stations but they are well known hard weather migrants, as too is the Black-headed Gull.

Cold winters are particularly difficult for birds dependent on access to open water, such as Kingfishers, because their food supply is then likely to be cut off by sheets of ice. Rosemary Eastman, in her book on the Kingfisher, summarises the historical data on this point: in 1889 the freezing of the Kennet near Newbury resulted in frozen Kingfishers being picked up daily along its banks; in the harmful winter of 1939/40 all but one or two Kingfisher pairs along a 68-mile stretch of the Thames were lost from a population originally in excess of 120 pairs; and the 1962/63 winter also saw heavy mortality. With less severe winters the birds leave the frozen streams and rivers and move down to estuaries to feed on shrimps and other crustaceans. Kingfishers in Britain are a relatively sedentary species, but on the Continent the regularity of severe winters has turned the species into a migrant, birds moving south and west out of the more northern European countries before the rivers freeze.

Excessively severe winters can cause physical injuries to birds. The severe winters of 1978/79 and 1981/82 produced many observations of birds injured by frost or severe cold. One GBFS observer in Dorset found that many of his birds were lame during the cold spells of the winter, and that shallow baths of hot water which he put out to enable them to thaw snowballs from their feet were much appreciated. In Cambridge, another observer found that several of

159

Aggression on the riverbank

The Pied Wagtail appears to suffer particular hardship in freezing conditions, with even quite short spells of such weather leading to increased mortality. A study of the birds' behaviour along the banks of the River Thames during winter reveals something of the reasons behind this. The wagtails feed mainly on small flies, spiders and beetles, picking these up along the edge of the river where flying insects that have fallen into the water are washed up on to the bank. Without the current flowing this source of food is denied to the birds.

Wagtails actually show complex feeding behaviour related to this food supply. Individual birds defend territories along the riverbank because once they have eaten the insects available at a particular point on the bank it will be some time before enough insects are washed up at that point for it to be worth while continuing to feed there. Thus the wagtail progresses along its stretch of the bank, feeding in places where sufficient insects have accumulated to provide a meal. The bird then returns to its starting point and searches through the area again, feeding on the freshly accumulated insects. There is obviously a risk that other wagtails may attempt to feed on that stretch of the bank before the owner returns, in which case they will be vigorously chased away. Other species which also feed on these insects, such as Meadow Pipit, Robin and Skylark, are all chased away too, but those whose diet does not overlap with that of the Pied Wagtail are not evicted. This may seem extraordinarily clever, but when one realises that a wagtail must find an insect every three or four seconds throughout a winter day to avoid losing weight it is easy to appreciate the strength of the pressures towards evolving such behaviour.

his birds had lost a leg, presumably due to frostbite. From Dumfries-shire a third observer recorded that at least three birds – two Black-birds and a Chaffinch – had lost their tails, being frozen in a roost at night or when feeding.

This at first sight anecdotal evidence of physical injury is suppor-ted by more systematic studies conducted by professional scientists. In the United States one researcher found that the incidence of frost on birds' plumage was related to their dominance status within the flock: those birds which were dominant secured the best, that is, the warmest places within the roost, forcing subordinate birds to remain nearer the edge of the roost where conditions were not so favourable. It was these birds that suffered frosting.

In Britain, too, studies of the behaviour of Rooks on roosting sites have shown that the older and more experienced adults, those which are also the dominant individuals in the roost, secure places further into the roost trees where shelter from cold winds is greatest. The immature birds of the year are forced to take the more exposed positions in the upper branches of the trees. Of course, there must be some compensating advantage to being in an inferior position within these roosts or the young ones would do better by going away and forming a roost of their own somewhere else (unless suitable roosting areas are in short supply). One possibility is that in the big traditional roosts of this species it is the older, more experienced birds who know where the best sources of food may be found at each stage of the winter, and, by roosting alongside them, the inexperien-ced youngsters can obtain more food than they would if they had to search for it on their own (see p. 155).

162

10 Garden hazards

A sad but unalterable fact is that most birds die young. Almost every wild bird faces a very wide range of day-to-day risks, and it is the hope of everyone who feeds birds in the garden to reduce these risks to a minimum. As already noted in Chapter 2, complete protection is not only impossible but undesirable, but it is as well to 'know your enemy' in order that steps may be taken to keep its depredations under control.

Domestic animals

Cats

Of all birds' enemies the domesticated cat must be placed first. Its behaviour is perfectly natural, but man domesticated the cat and it is neither the cats' nor the birds' fault that all too often they find themselves together in your garden. There are three main courses of action open to anyone with a cat problem who wishes to feed and encourage birds to nest safely in the garden. These are careful planning, active discouragement and, perhaps surprisingly, keeping one's own cat or dog.

Planning the garden boundaries to exclude, as far as possible, the larger predatory mammals has already been discussed, but there are also certain precautions which one can take within the garden. Siting the various feeding areas needs careful attention. The cat's usual method of hunting birds is to remain hidden and perfectly still until its quarry approaches close enough for it to be caught in a single

The Cuckoo arrives during April from its winter quarters in Africa and proves a unique hazard in gardens. The parasitic female may lay as many as twenty-five eggs in different nests, unwitting hosts ranging in size from Wren to Blackbird. This young Cuckoo was raised by a Dunnock – the commonest and most successful host in British gardens – fewer being reared by Robins, Pied Wagtails and Spotted Flycatchers.

The cunning cat

Some cats, particularly Siamese, are adept at taking birds in flight, concealing themselves on a windowsill or a shed roof and pouncing upon birds flying to or from the bird table, even taking Swifts and Swallows in this way. One particular cat formed the habit of climbing an ivy-covered tree to spring upon the birds feeding on the table below. Even if the table itself is safe, and this can be achieved either by using a smooth metal or plastic covered pole or by training a closely pruned rambler rose around a wooden pole, the area immediately below the table is still a vulnerable spot, for many birds will descend there to feed upon the bits of food which fall to the ground.

leap, so it is essential that all food should be at least 5 metres from cover of any kind. Remember, too, that the unfolding of foliage and the growth of vegetation in spring can be very rapid, so that a site which was perfectly safe at the end of February can be a death trap by the middle of March.

Cats are a great hazard to birds in the nesting season, so the siting of nestboxes is as important as the positioning of the various feeding stations. In this case the hazards are twofold: the adult birds may be at risk when approaching or leaving the box, or they may be so alarmed at the presence of the cat as to reduce the feeding of the nestlings to a dangerous level, resulting in the ultimate death of the brood. There is also the possibility that the parents may give up the unequal struggle and desert the site. In gardens where there are cats, therefore, the position of each nestbox must be considered with great care. On a bare wall a height of about 3 metres should be sufficient, but beware of convenient ledges, sheds, fence-tops or overhanging branches which might be used as a springboard by the cat. On posts or a tree trunk the erection of an inverted cone of metal (see p. 169) or wire netting beneath the box may foil the animal's attempts to climb, or a bundle of thorny branches of holly, hawthorn or gorse may serve the same purpose, while the practice of planting similar thorny subjects around the base of potential nesting trees has much to recommend it.

Discouragement is never easy, especially when the cat has discovered that birds are often there for the taking, as they are at a feeding station or an occupied nestbox. If the animal is an undoubted stray the RSPCA can be called to remove it, but for one's own or the neighbour's cats alternative methods have to be used, none of which can be guaranteed to be entirely effective. There are proprietary compounds on the market which are supposed to deter cats; some may work for a limited period, but constant renewal is necessary to produce any lasting effect. Pepper is useful, for example to protect a newly planted seed bed, but one can hardly scatter pepper around the whole garden. It is expensive, and will also need to be replaced each morning following rain or a heavy dew. As short-term deterrents in an emergency, shouting, clapping or waving the washing may serve the purpose, for cats quickly learn when their presence is not welcome, but for lasting effect something more memorable is required. Windfall apples, conkers or an old tennis ball hurled in the right direction rarely hit their target but do serve to reinforce the meaning of the shout which invariably accompanies them. Water is by far the best of the harmless deterrents if one can get near enough to use it. A well-aimed polythene bag or a plastic squash bottle filled with water and lobbed beside the cat – from upstairs perhaps – will explode and shower thoroughly, and a well-directed jet from the garden hose is equally effective.

At first sight owning one's own cat might appear to increase the problem rather than solving it, but cats are territorial animals and if there is no cat in residence the garden is likely to be treated as common ground by neighbouring cats from far and wide. Toms are less of a problem than queens; a female cat in season will attract a vociferous horde of admirers, and females are much more likely to develop into compulsive hunters than toms, so the best choice would be a neutered male who is unlikely to wander far from home. He should be provided with a collar and a bell at a very early age to warn birds of his approach.

The scent marks left by the resident cat will do much to ward off neighbouring cats even when the resident animal is indoors. This is a great advantage over other forms of deterrent, which usually depend on the garden owner being present to operate them. For the same reason a cat is probably a rather better deterrent than a dog, since the dog is only effective when he is free to patrol the garden, and in the early hours of the morning when most needed he will probably be curled up in his basket. Of course, if the garden is a large one and the dog can be allowed to roam freely at all times the local cat population is hardly likely to be allowed to remain long enough to form bad habits.

Ferrets

Of the other domesticated animals only an escaped ferret presents a real danger, for this can destroy all the nest contents within a wide area and even make inroads into the adult birds at roost during the winter. The assistance of a gamekeeper to trap or shoot the offender is the best solution; he will probably be able to produce a ferret of the opposite sex to act as a lure.

Wild animals

Some of the wild animals which may visit the bird garden may be as much a source of enjoyment to the owner as the birds. Most are harmless; a few, if they stumble across a nest by chance, will eat the contents, either eggs or young; two, the wood mouse and the weasel, can be extremely destructive once they have discovered that nest-boxes represent potential food sources, and the grey squirrel and the rat are pests to be discouraged whenever possible.

Red squirrel

Few gardeners are likely to be worried by the activities of the native red squirrel since it is now a very locally distributed British mammal and, as such, if it appears in the occasional favoured garden, should be afforded all the protection the bird gardener would bestow upon his feathered guests. To be strictly fair, its habits are little better than those of its grey cousin, but as a declining species it is far more in need of protection than any of the birds whose nests it may plunder, or whose food it may steal from the bird table. The measures adopted to protect the food provided for birds against the onslaughts of the grey squirrel will be described later; the less drastic of these may serve against the red, but perhaps the best advice would be to double the quantity of nuts provided, feed the squirrel away from the main bird feeding areas and rejoice in its presence.

Dormice

Two other potential rascals, the native dormouse and the introduced edible dormouse which is at present confined to a small part of central Southern England, should also be tolerated, even welcomed, on the same grounds – that of scarcity. Their nests, distinctive balls of leaves, may be used solely as a resting place or they may raise young in them. Minimal disturbance to find out whether the nest is occupied by gently teasing apart the ball with a twig should ensure that breeding is not disturbed. During the winter the native species generally builds its own hibernaculum in a hazel thicket, but either species may decide to move indoors to a shed or loft – if the latter

Red Squirrels are a welcome addition to any bird table but, like their grey cousins, they consume large quantities of expensive food. Genuinely squirrel-proof wire nut containers are available, and if you wish you can restrict squirrels' activities on the bird table with wire mesh.

is chosen the slumbers of the owner may be disturbed by stored apples being rolled across the bedroom ceiling in the small hours of the morning. Both species may be guilty of taking an occasional egg or young bird, or of helping themselves to a few nuts from the bird table, but their very scarcity will ensure that these depredations are not serious.

Mice

The most destructive of all small rodents is the wood mouse or long-tailed field mouse. In areas equipped with large numbers of nest-boxes up to 95 per cent of the eggs or young of the occupied nests have been taken in a single season. Direct control is not possible because the extent of the destruction depends upon population levels which cannot be foreseen, but Jack Fox, of the Hereford and Radnor Naturalists' Trust, has come up with an ingenious and promising solution. As soon as an attack is indicated he uses the waxy anti-mouse pellets sold by Sutton's the seedmerchants; these, pressed into the bark of the tree around the nest or the nestbox, have proved highly successful and he has not suffered a serious outbreak of nestbox predation by wood mice since.

Distinguishing the dormice

Dormice are easily recognised. The British species (right) has a chestnut coat, prominent black eyes, large ears and a thickly furred long tail which, together with the habit of sitting on its haunches while eating food, give it the appearance of a tiny squirrel. The edible dormouse is much larger, and grey, with a piratical dark patch on the face. In addition to its misdeeds in the garden it is also accused of doing a certain amount of damage to forestry plantations. It is probably a good thing if this introduced species retains its rarity status; as a common animal it could develop into a major pest.

Other small rodents are unlikely to harm the birds, but if they gain access to the bird food store they can prove extremely expensive. Bulk foods (seeds, nuts, etc.) should always be stored in animal- and insect-proof containers – screwtop glass or plastic jars for small quantities, steel bins or big tins for the large-scale operator. In addition to what they eat, mice will carry away and store incredible quantities of food in a single night, and they will take almost anything which is offered to the birds: nuts, wheat, seeds, acorns, peas and beans – nothing comes amiss, and they will continue to take it away as long as supplies last, poking items into the most unlikely places. Mice will also climb up to and remove food from the bird table during the night, but in this case they themselves become potential food items for the local owls. It is essential, too, that the lids of the containers fit properly, not only to exclude the mice but to keep out the winter moths. These will lay their eggs among the food and the larvae do untold damage, especially if the food is to be kept throughout the summer months.

Other visitors

The larger mammals may also take advantage of the free meals provided for the birds, and one hears increasingly of people who illuminate the areas around the feeding table in order to watch these nocturnal visitors. Foxes, hedgehogs and even badgers may become regulars, and if not disturbed they soon learn to ignore any human activity behind the window. Hedgehogs are almost entirely beneficial in the garden, and a saucerful of bread and milk placed in the same spot every evening will soon have them coming regularly. Their normal diet is slugs, snails and other garden undesirables, but if they blunder into a nest of Robin's eggs or young, these will go too.

Though the hedgehog is not a determined nest hunter he is an omnivorous opportunist. A box designed by Lawrence D. Hills of the Henry Doubleday Foundation specifically for hedgehogs may encourage them to remain around the garden. They may even rear a litter there, but care should be taken never to burn a heap of leaves in the garden without first shaking it out to make certain that it has not become the home of a hedgehog, for this is his normal choice.

If the garden is to be a refuge for all wild creatures, bats will be welcome, and they, too, can be provided with boxes in which they may breed, or a roost in a roof space may be occupied. Bat enthusiasts from the Mammal Society are always pleased to hear of colonies of bats and will often come to see and identify them, and if asked, offer advice. Populations of many species appear to be declining, so bats around the garden should be looked upon as a blessing – and they NEVER get caught in human hair.

British snakes are harmless enough. Even the adder is unlikely to attack anyone except the gardener who makes a practice of creeping around the garden barefoot; at the approach of a normal heavy-footed human it will usually slip away unseen. All snakes will eat an occasional egg or young bird, but like the hedgehog they are not inveterate nest hunters.

Mammalian malefactors

There remain three mammals for which few excuses can be made – a persistent problem for the dedicated bird gardener – the brown rat, the weasel and the grey squirrel. Of the three, the last is probably the one which causes the most trouble in those areas which it has now colonised, for not only will the grey squirrel eat eggs and young birds, it will take over a large nestbox, consume almost anything provided for the birds and, if it cannot get the food in any other way, carry away the food container and work away with its razor-sharp teeth until the contents are exposed. Squirrel-proofing is very difficult. Shooting is obviously the most effective, and is legal provided that humans are not endangered and the gun is more than 50 feet from the middle of any road. The all wire 'live' rat trap is effective, but one then has the problem of dealing with the catch. The bird table should be well away from nearby trees, and the metal cone used against cats may prevent squirrels from climbing the pole, but perhaps the most successful deterrent of all is to stretch a stout wire between two trees and suspend the feeding tray from the centre of this. Grey squirrels will still perform a tight-rope act along the horizontal wire and attempt to slide down the vertical wire, but another metal cone half way down the latter should foil them.

Various hanging feeders are on the market, and all should be fitted with anti-squirrel cones if these animals become a problem.

The weasel can become a serious cause for concern in a garden equipped with a large number of nestboxes. Like the Blue Tits which discovered that a bottle with a negotiable tinfoil cap contained cream, and that the bottles with golden tops had even better cream, or the Grey Herons which now realise that there is often good food in ponds in suburban gardens, weasels in some areas have become aware that rectangular boxes fixed to tree trunks or walls are potential food reservoirs. If this problem occurs it is a mistake to use a number of boxes of a similar pattern in a restricted area; boxes should be of a variety of types, and every effort should be made at disguise by placing them in the brushwood sprouting from a tree trunk, behind the climbing rose on a wall or on a post thrust into the centre of a thick, thorny berberis. If an outbreak of trouble from a weasel begins in a garden which was formerly free it might be advisable to trap and dispose of the offender. An almost totally weasel-proof nestbox, of composition concrete for strength, suspended from a wire and with a smooth cone on top, is now in use at Wytham woods, near Oxford.

Brown rats spend much of the summer in the fields and hedge banks, but in winter they prefer to move into barns, ricks, outbuildings or garden sheds – anywhere dry – and if there is a readily available supply of food at hand, so much the better. This is the time that bird feeding establishments are at risk. Rats, like grey squirrels, will eat almost anything, and as with squirrels, every effort should be made to get rid of them. Most local councils employ a Rodent Operator (he used to be called a rat catcher) who can be called in if the outbreak is serious; traps set *inside* the closed shed or beneath its floorboards, well away from inquisitive Robins and Blackbirds, will cope with the itinerant individual, while a nestbox for Tawny Owls also has its use. Small bore rifles and a good terrier dog also have their advocates. Old, smelly fish heads, unattractive to birds, make an excellent bait for rat traps.

Bird predators

In addition to attack from ground level birds are also at risk from the air. Hawks and owls will take the adult birds; Carrion Crows, Magpies, Jays and to a lesser extent Jackdaws will take either eggs or young birds from the nests, and Great Spotted Woodpeckers will attack and hack open nestboxes for the same purpose. This last, deplorable habit is of fairly recent origin; it is discussed at greater length on p. 174.

Hawks

Birds naturally tend to gather where food is readily available and the Sparrowhawk is no exception, so the feeding station with its numerous small birds will inevitably prove attractive. While it may be distressing to witness a kill actually at the bird table there is relatively little one can – or should – do about it, for if the kill does not take place there it will certainly do so not very far away and the same bird population will provide the victim. At one feeding station the entire feeding area is enclosed so that the small birds can get in and the hawk cannot, but even here the hawk is likely to alight on top of the enclosure and the small birds, terrified at its presence, will almost certainly attempt to leave the safety of the cage in time and make for the nearest cover.

Some hindrance to Sparrowhawks can be achieved by keeping the feeding area well away from obvious flight lines along which the predator can approach. The vicinity of tall hedges and the edges of woodland should be avoided, so that the potential victims at least have some warning as the hawk covers those important few yards

Sparrowhawk breeding success and population numbers have increased since the pesticides era (see p. 84), and birds appear in gardens, especially in autumn and winter, dashing into a flock of feeding birds or dropping on to individuals. Their kills can be restricted by covering ground feeding areas and bird tables with chicken wire.

171

Death from above

A Kestrel in the New Forest became a Blue Tit specialist, taking its victims from a ringer's bird table. From the pellets around its roost no fewer than 34 rings were recovered over the four winters between 1975/76 and 1978/79, and no doubt this was only the tip of the iceberg; many unringed birds would undoubtedly have been taken as well. But it is unlikely that the Blue Tit population in the New Forest was seriously depleted by the Kestrel's activities.

of open ground, but it is unrealistic to imagine that because he failed to kill at the bird table the Sparrowhawk will go to roost hungry. Even if predation builds up during cold weather it is still better to continue to feed the small birds, for starvation will account for far more of them than the hawk is ever likely to do.

The presence of a Kestrel around the rural garden is less often a problem since its normal diet usually comprises the smaller rodents, beetles and larger insects. However, occasional individuals work out a successful technique for catching birds in quantity, especially urban Kestrels feeding on House Sparrows and Starlings.

Birds of prey

observed at GBFS sites during the 1970s, chasing or killing avian prey within feeding station or taking meat and bones

Species	No. of stations visited	Combined weekly peak counts	No. of winters raptor recorded
Sparrowhawk	70	489	10
Kestrel	28	354	10
Tawny Owl	9	318	8
Little Owl	3	22	2
Merlin	3	20	6
Barn Owl	2	4	2
Buzzard	1	2	2
Great Grey Shrike	1	1	1

Data from 723 sites. In other rural gardens Red Kite, Hen Harrier, Goshawk and Peregrine have been recorded.

Owls

Predation by owls is probably under-recorded since most of it takes place either at dusk or at first light. Tawny Owls in the parks and gardens of our larger towns and cities take a number of small birds, usually House Sparrows and Starlings, and the Little Owl, which frequently hunts by day as well as by night, also includes both adult birds and fledglings in its diet. Several cases of Tawnies visiting bird tables have been reported, but a number of these reports suggest that the main attraction in these cases was the bones and meat put out for the smaller birds rather than the birds themselves.

Crows

One of the most distressing aspects of garden bird protection is the predation of nests by members of the crow family, the corvids. The Carrion Crow, Magpie and Jay are the three worst offenders; the Rook and the Jackdaw will take any eggs or young birds which they come across during their normal feeding forays – a clutch of Lapwing eggs or a brood of young Skylarks in the grass – but they are not dedicated nest hunters as is the case with the first three species. Many years ago the activities of gamekeepers assisted in keeping the number of all three under control, for the keepers were well aware of the depredations of these birds, and as a result rural areas remained thinly populated and there was no cause for the spread into suburban and even urban areas which has taken place in recent years and which continues today.

Some idea of the extent of the damage which the Carrion Crow can do may be gained by examining the ground beneath the nest of a pair with half-grown young; it can be littered with the discarded shells of eggs including Mallard, Grey Partridge, Pheasant, Moorhen, Coot, Lapwing, domestic poultry and many more. There will, of course, be no evidence of the number of nestlings which have also been consumed, and if the eggshells of the smaller birds are missing, that is simply because they have been swallowed or fed to the nestling crows whole. Shooting rogue birds early in the year is the only effective remedy, but the destruction of any nests under construction in the vicinity of the garden is worthwhile because the ravages are at their worst when the corvines themselves have a brood to rear. The raids are usually made very early in the morning, when a pair of Magpies will systematically search out every nest within their territory, and the contents of many within the garden will be plundered; then, for a few days there will be no further visits while the birds deal with other sections of their territory, but after a lapse of a week or ten days when new nests have appeared and fresh clutches have been laid, the whole process is repeated.

Redstart nests in hollow trees into which crows can reach may be protected by tacking or wiring a wire mesh strip across the entrance, with the base of one mesh level with the lower part of the cavity (see opposite). On one occasion the partially decomposed body of a Jay was discovered jammed upside down in the cavity. Beneath that was the body of a female Redstart, and beneath her, a nest with seven eggs. A strip of wire netting might have saved both adult birds from a particularly horrible death. Old wire netting, somewhat rusty but still strong, is best, particularly if it is to be used in public places where new netting might attract attention.

Great Spotted Woodpecker

It is a pity that the last of the avian predators should have to be a most attractive garden bird, but there is no doubt that the Great Spotted Woodpecker does, in some areas, qualify for the status of 'problem' bird. Possibly its habit of attacking nestboxes began with it investigating the box as a potential nest site, but Great Spotted Woodpeckers now attack for one purpose only – to get at, and eat, the eggs or young of the rightful occupants. There is little one can do to protect a wooden box which already contains a tit's nest, and in all probability the tits will have deserted long before the woodpecker has achieved his objective, but new boxes of composition

A despairing pair of Blue Tits can do little themselves to stop a Great Spotted Woodpecker gaining access and devouring the nest contents, but you can adopt various measures to prevent such losses.

Protection for the small birds

Very little can be done to protect the open nests of many garden species such as Dunnocks, Robins, Blackbirds and thrushes, but some success has been achieved using 2 inch (5 cm) mesh wire netting to cover the nests of really tiny birds. A conical ornament conifer containing the nest of a Goldcrest was completely wrapped in this useful material through which the Goldcrest passed, apparently without noticing it was there. The nest of a Willow Warbler had a tent of netting pegged down around it, and the nest of a pair of Redstarts in a rusty five gallon petrol can in the bracken (left) had an apron of the same material stretched across the gaping rust hole with equal success.

concrete, plastic or metal would discourage further attacks. If metal boxes are used they must always be hung in the shade. A better alternative is to use wooden boxes with the joints protected by metal strips and the hole by a sheet metal plate, formica or rubber sheeting. The provision of adequate quantities of fat on which the birds will feed their young might, if the supply is maintained, help to keep the woodpecker's mind off other possible food sources.

Man-made hazards

No gardener would knowingly destroy a nest, but great care is needed during the breeding season to ensure that accidents are avoided. Bundles of pea or bean sticks are frequently adopted by Dunnocks or Blackbirds, particularly early in the season before the hedges and shrubs provide adequate cover. These should always be examined carefully before the bundle is moved. Open sheds and outbuildings are extremely popular, and the nests within them may be very well concealed so the careless shifting of a stepladder, a roll of wire netting or an old coat may well bring a shower of eggs around the ears of the gardener. Care must be taken, too, to see that the doors or windows of such buildings are never accidentally left closed. The garden bonfire needs attention; nests may be deserted if the shrubs containing them are scorched or subjected to smoke over a long period. Hedge cutting is best left until late in the year, for Greenfinches often have occupied nests until early September and the leaving of a small area of cover around an occupied nest only serves to draw attention to it.

The actual design of the house may place birds at risk, for every year large numbers of birds die through hitting glass (usually windows or doors), while others collide with wires and a vast number are killed on the roads. At first sight road accidents may not appear to be a matter for consideration in a book on the garden, but a thoughtlessly sited feeder near a hedgerow beside a busy road may easily lead to the deaths of the very birds one is trying to help, struck down as they cross the road to reach it. Overhead wires are not an important hazard to most small garden bird species, but if gulls come into the area in cold weather they are at risk if the lawn is traversed by telephone or electricity wires. In some cases where casualties do occur British Telecom or the Electricity Board may be persuaded to put corks or plastic markers on the wires to make them more conspicuous to the birds.

Glass is a more difficult problem, and one which affects a variety of species, large and small, diurnal and nocturnal. Two types of accident occur, the one caused by reflection, the other because the victim thinks that it can see a clear way through the glass and out into the open country on the other side. A picture window through the lounge, a conservatory, a greenhouse, or in its simplest form a door or window opening outwards may all produce this effect, and the complete powder imprint of a Tawny Owl, with every feather visible, on the lounge window is all that is needed to show that even the sharp-eyed nocturnal birds can be duped in this way. For the greenhouse a light coating of whitewash or commercial greenhouse shading may be all that is required, but for the glass around the house this is not usually acceptable. Here net curtains or a climbing plant allowed to hang down in front of the window may be effective, or the silhouette of a Sparrowhawk fixed to the window may also serve. If the bird is flying into the glass because of a reflection the curtain or the silhouette would have to be on the outside of the glass.

At night bright lights may attract birds to the window but this is not a common problem in Britain. In some parts of North America hundreds of small birds are killed against the lighted windows of skyscrapers on damp, misty nights during the migration season, but there are few such records in Britain.

Birds apparently stunned or showing signs of uncoordinated movement as a result of such accidents should be placed in a cardboard box in a warm place for an hour or two. If the bird then appears to have recovered it should be liberated in the garden — never indoors, where it will almost certainly fly into another window and kill itself. If the injuries are more serious the animal welfare organisations may be able to help, or there may be someone locally with experience in dealing with such cases.

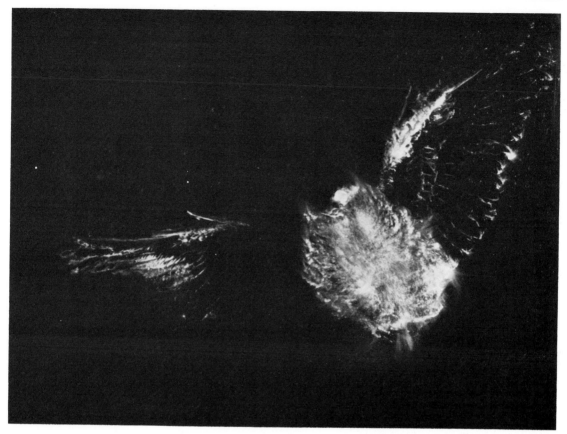

For many birds collision with a window is fatal. This one, probably a pigeon or dove, left its imprint on the windowpane but escaped with its life. Such 'impactograms' are quite frequently recorded, particularly concerning pigeons, doves and owls.

If the bird dies it may still be of interest to someone. There are post-mortem investigations run nationally on a variety of species which are subject to change from time to time, and details are generally announced through the RSPB publication *Birds*, and through *BTO News*. Local museums are often pleased to have even the commoner species, and the ringing office of the BTO would, of course, like all such birds to be checked for rings and the data – place, cause of death, date, species of bird and the finder's name and address – to be forwarded to Tring.

11 Studying garden birds

The practice of feeding garden birds is probably more widespread in Britain than in any other country, and it undoubtedly helps a large number of our resident birds and those winter visitors which are prepared to accept our offerings to survive through periods of hard weather. For many people this is sufficient; they are content to feel that they are contributing to the well-being of the birds and have no burning desire to know more about them. Others may become fascinated by some aspect of their behaviour and feel that they would like to know a little more about it.

Ways of attracting birds into the garden have been discussed in earlier chapters, and the individual requirements of the various species have also received attention. If the birds are to be encouraged to remain throughout the spring and summer, food becomes of secondary importance; the first need is for a suitable place to nest, where the birds will be undisturbed and protected from predators and to some extent, weather.

Robins often occupy nest sites deliberately or accidentally provided by man. This bird is feeding its brood in an old tin can; other favoured situations include kettles or coal buckets wedged in tree forks, tweed coat pockets, or bundles of pea-sticks strategically placed in the shed corner.

Natural nesting sites

Open-nesting birds – that is those such as thrushes and finches, which do not normally nest in holes or crevices – will be attracted to thick hedges, shrubs and trees. If these are already growing in the garden they should be maintained as thick cover and not allowed to become too straggly. Hedges of thorny species such as hawthorn and blackthorn are especially valuable as they deter predators more effectively. Some open-nesting species will nest in very prominent positions; the Mistle Thrush often chooses the bare fork of a tall tree

179

and relies on its bold, aggressive nature to drive away its enemies. In contrast, many of the small birds such as warblers, buntings and some of the finches prefer to nest fairly close to the ground, and a secluded corner of the garden, overgrown with brambles, nettles and other dense vegetation, is the most likely place to attract a Whitethroat, Blackcap, Willow Warbler, Linnet or Yellowhammer.

Another group of species, although building nests similar in style to those of the open-nesters, prefers to place them in a crevice rather than in a tree or bush. It is difficult to contrive sites for these. If they nest in a garden they frequently choose a site which the owner never even considered as a possibility, like the bowl of the electric light in a poultry house which served as a home for Pied Wagtails or the depression in the top of a roll of wire netting used by Spotted Flycatchers. It is worthwhile leaving a pile of brushwood in the corner of a shed or garage – remembering to leave a permanently open space for the birds to come and go – and an old coat hanging in a dark corner is often sufficient for a Wren or a Robin.

Gaps in brick walls, especially those overgrown with honey-suckle, ivy or some other trailing plant, are ideal for this group, and

A typical nest site for Swallows is on the rafters and joists of an outbuilding, where they make an open mud and straw cup nest, lined with grass and feathers. The nest needs a little support, which can be a narrow ledge. Garages and sheds will be used where there is constant access via a door or window during the summer. This bird nested in a coil of wire hung up in an outside lavatory.

Blue Tits nest in cavities and choose the most unusual sites. This brood are almost ready to emerge from their nest in the headlamp space of an old lorry.

if you have a stream running at the bottom of the garden you may be fortunate enough to attract a Grey Wagtail to such a site. Old kettles or tin cans lying half hidden in the herbage are popular; it is impossible to predict what species will find such sites to their liking. In one area where the houses had rather long drives the owners placed long, horizontal boxes on the gateposts for the convenience of the boy delivering the papers. At the end of May one of these gateposts had two boxes – which seemed a little unnecessary. Furtive examination early in the morning revealed that the original box contained a brood of Redstarts, and it was nice to see that both the owner and the boy with the newspapers were respecting the interests of the squatters!

The third group of species are those which nest in holes. Suitable sites for these are usually far more limited than those for the previous groups, and one can obviously help here by putting up nestboxes. These birds will of course also use a variety of natural or man-made sites which were not strictly intended for their use. Jackdaws can be a nuisance if they decide to nest in a chimney, for the quantity of sticks they will drop into a cavity until it is filled to their satisfaction can be enormous; Starlings and House Sparrows, and occasionally tits, may block the downpipe of the guttering if the entrances are not covered with wire domes, but the point is that few of these difficulties would arise if suitable natural sites were available.

Finding a hole to nest in

Ancient elm trees formerly provided many such sites for hole-nesting birds. Barn and Tawny Owls (right), Stock Doves and Jackdaws used the larger cavities, and woodpeckers hacked holes in the decaying branches – holes which would later serve as homes for tits, Nuthatches or Starlings, while Treecreepers were satisfied with the crannies under the loose bark. The felling of several million elms in the 1970s following the outbreak of Dutch elm disease has robbed all these birds of potential nesting sites, and in some cases it is probably the lack of such sites which is responsible for the scarcity of certain species rather than shortage of food or the unsuitability of the habitat. Experiments have shown that the tit population in coniferous woods can be considerably increased simply through the provision of suitable nestboxes, and Pied Flycatchers have been likewise persuaded to increase their range.

Artificial nest sites—nestboxes

So providing nestboxes of various types can be of considerable assistance to the birds. It is also invaluable to the student of birds, since in many cases it is impossible to examine the nest contents of a hole-nesting species in a natural site. With a nestbox careful examination throughout the nesting season will enable the observer to note progress, and an accurate record of the complete cycle of events can be achieved. Research biologists have used boxes on a large scale to carry out studies into the population dynamics of a variety of birds including Tawny Owls, Kestrels, Pied Flycatchers and tits. Nestboxes have also been used successfully for conservation purposes where mature woodland has been felled, for even if these areas are replanted immediately, it will be many years before the trees are large enough to provide the necessary holes, and in many cases the replanting is largely of coniferous trees which are not particularly given to producing the necessary cavities until they are fully mature.

The same problem arises in the garden. Very few small gardens can provide old trees, for these are likely to have been removed for the convenience of the builder. Although ground cover and hedges and shrubs can be provided fairly rapidly, only time will produce a tree with a massive trunk in which an owl can find a home – and most gardens are not large enough to hold such a tree.

Nestboxes with small round entrance holes are the type most commonly seen. These boxes can be found in most garden shops, but they are not always very well designed. A common mistake is to have the entrance hole much too close to the cup of the nest, so that a cat or a squirrel can insert a paw and scoop out the contents. The distance between these two points is just as important as the internal dimensions, although this too, particularly in drilled-out natural birch log boxes, is frequently inadequate.

The smaller species of titmice will nest in boxes only 7.5 cm square – some natural Coal Tit sites may be even smaller – but to be on the safe side a home-made box should never be smaller than 10 cm square internally. The distance between the bottom of the entrance hole and the base of the box must always be at least 12.5 cm. Not that the birds object to having a larger box; one pair of Great Tits nested in a child's discarded schooldesk, entering through the hole which should have held the ink well! The desk was completely full of moss – enough to fill a fair sized bucket – and the nest cup was a hair-lined depression in the corner opposite the hole. The young birds fledged successfully.

Making nestboxes

The top cutting diagram on p. 184 should be taken, therefore, as a pattern for a medium-sized box suitable for such species as tits, Nuthatches or sparrows. A smaller version will be preferred by both Marsh and Coal Tits, while Starlings need something rather larger (see the lower diagram on p. 184).

It is possible to exercise some control over the species which will use the box by regulating the size of the entrance hole. A hole of 2.7 cm ($1\frac{1}{16}$ in) diameter is a tight fit for a Blue Tit, but quite satisfactory for Marsh or Coal. One of 3.2 cm ($1\frac{1}{4}$ in) diameter will serve for Redstart, Pied Flycatcher, Great Tit, Nuthatch and Tree Sparrow, but if House Sparrows become a problem it may be necessary to reduce this to 2.9 cm ($1\frac{1}{8}$ in), which will exclude all but the most persistent House Sparrow. It is sometimes difficult to obtain a carpenter's bit of the exact measurement, but the problem can be overcome by using one a size smaller and enlarging the hole with a red hot poker or rounded carpenter's file.

When making a nestbox it is better to use screws than nails, but if nails are used they should be galvanised, as wire nails rust too easily. The lid should be fitted with a rustproof metal or plastic hinge, or a strip of leather running the full width of the box may be substituted. A sound catch to foil an inquisitive squirrel is essential. If the box is to hang in an exposed position it is a good plan to fix it to a 5 × 2.5 cm section batten. This will keep the back of the box clear

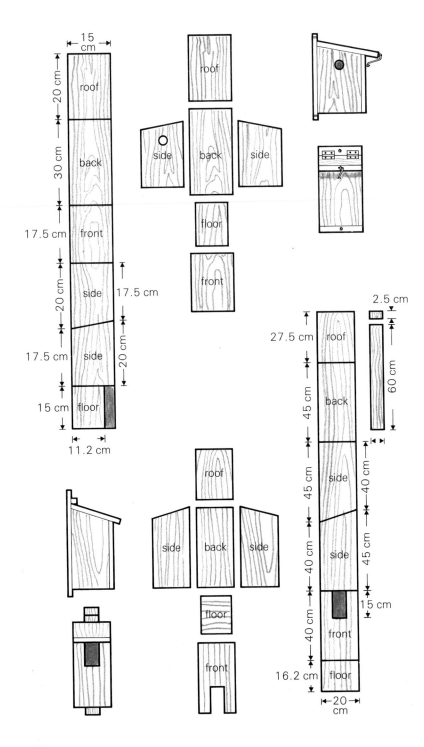

Left: The basic type of
nestbox design shown here
can be made in a small or
large format. The small
box (above: left, right and
centre) is the most
versatile, attracting over
fifteen species ranging from
Great Spotted Woodpecker
to Coal Tit. Its most likely
occupants in your garden
will be Great Tit, Blue Tit,
Starling or House Sparrow.
The large box (below: left,
right and centre) will also
prove attractive to
Starlings, but is designed
for larger species such as
Stock Dove and Jackdaw.
Birds are not particular
about the type of timber
used, and rough-sawn
planks are quite suitable.
These are often available
as $\frac{3}{4}$ inch (1.9 cm) planks,
in the width on which the
nestbox cutting diagrams
are based. You may need to
modify the dimensions
slightly to take into
account the thickness of the
timber used.

184

of the tree or wall on which it hangs, so that the rain will not collect between the box and its support. As with all other garden furniture, an annual application of a copper-based wood preservative is a good investment. This will not only prolong the life of the box, it will also deal effectively with any dormant parasites or their eggs or pupae which the previous occupants have left behind.

A similar box, but with an internal floor measurement of $20 \times 16.2\,\text{cm}$ and a depth of $25\,\text{cm}$ or more from the base of the entrance hole to the floor, is suitable for Stock Doves and Jackdaws.

Right: Specially designed artificial nests can be made for Swallows and House Martins from pottery clay, fibreglass or even coconut shells, using an old nest to give the dimensions of the mould. Clay must be fired in a kiln to withstand the weather. If you provide cup hooks as supports you can move the nest to inspect it. The lower diagram shows a special nestbox for Swifts, which should be placed just under the eaves by removing a brick in the outer wall.

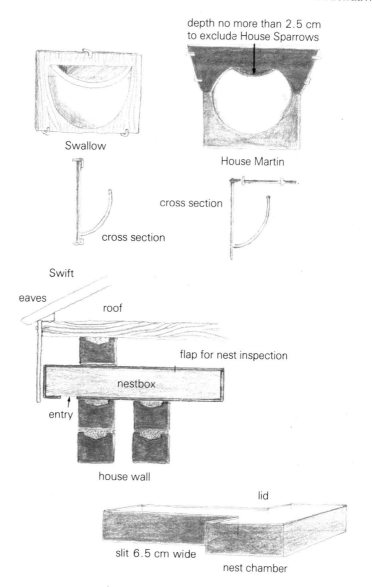

depth no more than 2.5 cm to exclude House Sparrows

Swallow

House Martin

cross section

cross section

Swift

eaves

roof

flap for nest inspection

nestbox

entry

house wall

lid

slit 6.5 cm wide

nest chamber

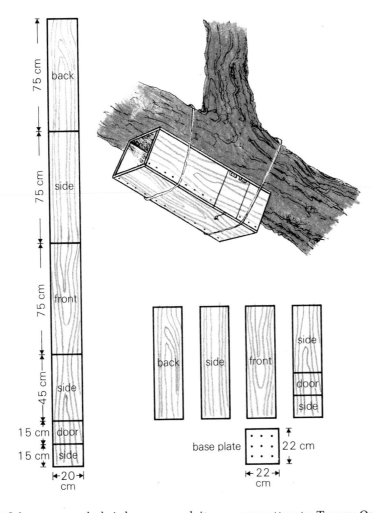

The 'chimney' type nestbox, resembling the broken-off branch of a tree, and positioned at an angle of about 30 degrees from the vertical, has been designed specifically for Tawny Owls and has proved very successful in attracting them. If possible erect the box during the autumn before the Tawny Owls claim their winter territories. A box may not be used by owls for a year or two, but in the meantime it may provide a welcome home for a pair of Stock Doves or Jackdaws.

If the entrance hole is large enough it may even attract a Tawny Owl, but for this species a special nestbox has been devised. Known as the chimney, it is meant to simulate the holes found in trees when a limb has broken off. It can be made quite simply by nailing together four wooden boards to form a square 'tube' 75 cm long and 20 cm square internally (see above). One end of the tube forms the base of the box and this should be fitted with a square baseplate of thin ferrous metal with at least six drainage holes, or perforated zinc; the other end remains open. A handful of sawdust, pine needles or peat will enable the bird to make a depression in which to lay the eggs, for owls do not build nests. The box should be hung at an angle of about 30 degrees from the vertical, usually at the junction of a large branch and the main trunk of the tree.

186

Erecting a nestbox for owls is not an operation to be undertaken lightly; two people are better than one, and careful preparation is necessary. Two really stout pieces of fence wire should be stapled to the front and sides of the box, leaving about 45 cm of free wire at each end to be fastened to the tree. One person can haul up the box by means of a rope passed over the branch of the tree, while his companion is on the ladder. It is sometimes easier to then tie the box in position with cord and attend to the stapling in comparative comfort. If you intend to inspect the inhabitants at a later date you should make certain that there is a door in the most convenient side or in the front. Not only is the box too deep to allow proper examination without such a door, but some owls are reluctant to leave and it is most unwise – even positively dangerous – to peer over the edge at a sitting bird. It should also be noted that some Tawny Owls take exception to being disturbed and may attack the intruder even after he has left the nest. An alternative method of examining the nest contents of high boxes is to fit a small adjustable mirror on a clamp over the entrance which can be positioned to give a clear view of the interior.

A useful box for those species which do not normally nest in holes – Pied Wagtail, Wren, Robin and Spotted Flycatcher – is the small open-fronted type. This is the same as the small hole box except that the front panel extends only half way up the box; the upper half remains completely open. If however you want to attract Spotted Flycatchers, all that is required is a completely open box 11 cm square internally and 4 cm deep placed amongst the creepers on a wall. Spotted Flycatchers insist on being able to see over the edge of the nest while they are incubating, so the open-fronted box is rather deeper than they need.

Positioning and hanging the nestboxes

In Britain much of the wet weather tends to come from between north-west and south-west and the strongest sun is in the south. In exposed positions, therefore, it is best to have the nestboxes facing from north through east to south-east. If there is adequate shelter and shade from nearby trees or buildings, aspect is unimportant.

The usual method of hanging a nestbox is to drill a small hole in the back and hang the box on a nail in the tree or wall. This means that the boxes invariably hang vertically, which may be unwise for two reasons. In the first place most climbing predators – cats, weasels, rats, even mice – have little difficulty in scaling these rough vertical surfaces. Secondly, and far more importantly, these same predators soon come to recognise the almost identical objects hanging in very similar positions as a potential source of food worthy of investigation, whether they are occupied or not. On several occasions large-scale experiments using nestboxes have had to be abandoned for this reason, and while it is unlikely that any one garden will be using boxes on this scale, several gardens in the same district may be doing so and the result will be much the same.

Natural cavities are not vertical; it matters little to the bird whether the nesting chamber is above or below the entrance hole and advantage can be taken of this to vary the hanging method for some of the boxes. One method is to have the hole in the end of the box and to strap the box to the underside of a nearly horizontal branch. In this position the entrance is protected by the branch immediately above it and the site closely resembles the broken-off end of a branch, a site which often meets with the approval of Redstarts. There is scope for experimenting with suspended boxes, for birds do not appear to object to a certain amount of movement and a box suspended by means of four wires would add considerably to the would-be predator's difficulties.

Some species are colonial in habit and several boxes can be placed in close proximity. House Martins, Jackdaws, Starlings and House Sparrows often nest in loose communities, while for Swifts the provision of two or more boxes side by side is almost essential unless there are other Swifts nesting nearby. For more strongly territorial small birds a density of 2–4 boxes per acre (5–10 per hectare) is often recommended, but remember that territorial rivalry only occurs between birds of the same or closely related species. Hence other species may occupy the newly installed boxes, and if there are migrant species in the district you do not want them to return to find all the nestboxes occupied by tits and Tree Sparrows. Far better in this case to have a box or two too many, even if they remain un-occupied for a season.

Christmas boxes

Most guides advise that boxes should be put up around Christmas or early in the New Year 'so that the birds can get used to them'. There is nothing wrong with this – the birds can use them for roosting purposes on cold winter nights when as many as a score or more of Wrens (right) may huddle into the same box – but do not let this deter you from erecting additional boxes, or boxes in a new garden in April or even early May. As often as not, the first prospecting tit will appear within twenty-four hours.

Most garden nestboxes with small hole entrances will be occupied by the local tits or sparrows. In some parts of the country, especially the north and west, Redstarts (right) may prove welcome occupants. By blocking the entrance hole of an empty box with a cork until the Pied Flycatchers arrive, another charming summer visitor can be helped.

Keeping the nestbox clean

Birds may be host to a number of parasites which spread from host to host by depositing their eggs in the old nests. These may infect the new arrivals when the nest cavity is next used, so it is advisable, except in the case of the Swift, to clean out the boxes every autumn. Do not be in too much of a hurry to do this, however; the young birds will frequently use the old nest site for roosting purposes for some time after they have vacated the nest. Swift nests are often heavily infested and should be treated with a suitable insecticide in September, as soon as the birds have departed. This gives the insecticide the maximum amount of time to perform its duties and to disperse.

Enjoying the results

Once the garden has been equipped with a variety of potential nesting sites success in inducing nesting is almost certain, and the owners of urban and suburban gardens should not be discouraged by the fact that some of the species we have mentioned do not appear to inhabit their gardens. It is surprising how many of our countryside and woodland birds can be found tucked away in quiet corners even in our larger cities. Parks and playing fields, the few remaining large old gardens, railway and canal embankments and churchyards, all may hold a few, and with the proper encouragement – food in the winter and nesting facilities in spring – there is no reason why some of them should not accept your hospitality. Birds nesting in gardens under the watchful eye of the owner present an ideal opportunity to record the full cycle of events, and the labour involved is very slight.

Keeping a nest record

The BTO has a specially designed Nest Record Card which is issued free of charge to anyone willing to complete and return it so that it may become part of the national collection. This is a long-running scheme which receives financial support from the Nature Conservancy Council; it started on a small scale in 1939 and now has an intake in excess of 20,000 cards per year. A card may be filled in for every nest containing eggs or young which is visited at least once, and inaccessible nests which are obviously being visited by the birds are also required since they provide details of nest site, habitat, etc. (see completed card). A few dedicated nest finders record larger numbers of nests every year, but records of single nests and those in and around the garden are particularly valuable since the continuity and completeness of the records is often much better than that achieved by the large-scale operators.

Full instructions appear on the back of the cards. There are spaces for the observer's name, species, year, county, location and altitude; once these have been completed all that is needed is the date of each observation and its finding. Some observers may, quite rightly, be a little concerned at the amount of disturbance the collection of this

OBSERVER R. A. MORGAN			SPECIES ROBIN			YEAR 19 **81**	B.T.O.Ref.
NO. of EGGS or YOUNG at each visit.			Record here stage of building; if bird sitting; if eggs warm; age of young; ring nos. etc.	COUNTY HERTS		If this record is entered on ATLAS CARD put ✓ in box	Office Use Only
DATE Day / Month	G.M.T.	EGGS	YNG.				D
2 APR				NEST ½ BUILT	LOCALITY (place-name) **B.T.O.** BEECH GROVE, TRING	Grid Ref	
12 APR				COMPLETE, LINED		SP932118	C
13 APR	1200	1		COLD			H
15 APR	1230	3		COLD	ALTITUDE above sea level **445** ....ft.		
18 APR	1300	5		WARM	HABITAT Delete those inapplicable:- RURAL/SUBURBAN/URBAN		F
30 APR	1100	1	4	NEWLY HATCHED	LARGE PRIVATE		
1 MAY			5	ADULT BROODING	GARDEN		
7 MAY			5	YOUNG RINGED			
14 MAY			4-5	FULLY FEATHERED			
16 MAY				NEST EMPTY	NEST SITE OPEN-FRONTED		
26 MAY				FLEDGED YOUNG	NEST BOX ON DEAD		
				SEEN NEARBY	BEECH STUMP		
Further visits, notes on outcome, etc. – ON BACK					Height above ground or cliff-base ....5...... ft.		

A completed Nest Record Card ready for return to the BTO's national collection.

data will entail, but with care and a little forethought this can be reduced to a minimum and no harm will result. There is no need, nor is it desirable, to visit a nest every day, although in the garden you may have to walk past the nest several times a day and it is often possible to see the sitting bird without disturbing it. If the occupant is not at home, it is an easy matter to take a quick look, count the contents and retire without the bird being aware of your visit. Birds are particularly sensitive in the early stages of the breeding cycle, and the earlier records should be marked 'B', indicating that the bird is building. No attempt should be made at this stage to examine the nest or even to locate it if it is hidden away in the hedge, but it is frequently possible to gain some idea of the progress by observing the nesting material which is being taken in; large bundles of coarse material suggest that building has only just commenced, the addition of hair, small feathers, etc. indicates that the final lining is being added, so the card entry might read 'April 30 . . . "B" (feathers)'. If you have a dog or cat, or if your children have a pony, groom it and put the hair in a wire nut container on the bird table; most small birds find this irresistible. (Do not put out the long hairs from the pony's tail. Birds can easily become entangled in it.)

Once building has finished and the carrying of nesting material has ceased, one or two afternoon visits will establish the date of the laying of the first egg. Most small birds lay one egg per day, early in the morning, until the clutch is complete, and incubation does not usually start until the evening before the last egg is to be laid, so it is unlikely that the bird will be sitting in the afternoon during the laying period. Having established the date of the first egg, no further visits are necessary for at least a week, or longer in the case of tits, which may have clutches of a dozen or more eggs. In the garden this inspection can often be made when the bird has been seen to leave the nest to feed, and by this time the clutch should be complete. If a nest already appears to have a full clutch, visit every 3–4 days for small passerines or 7–14 days for birds with a longer incubation period to give an approximate date of hatching.

Most garden nesting species have an incubation period of 12–14 days, so if you know the date of the first egg and the clutch size you already have a fair idea of when to expect the eggs to hatch. A careful watch at this time may reveal the bird carrying away an eggshell; if not, a quick inspection when the bird leaves the nest to feed should provide the information you need. It is often difficult to establish exactly how many young have hatched at this stage, and if the clutch is a large one no attempt should be made to do so; a tick in both the 'egg' and the 'young' column of the card is sufficient to indicate that hatching is in progress. The best time to record the number hatched is about three days after hatching. Before this time there is still the possibility that further eggs may hatch. The easiest time to count the young is when they are half grown: 6–7 days for most small birds, 9–11 days for tits and Swallows. It may still be possible to count the number of beaks in a nest for a further day or two, but this should only be done from a distance as there is now a danger that the young may take fright and 'explode' prematurely from the nest. Confirmation of successful fledging can often be recorded by watching the adult birds carrying food to the young which are now hidden away in various parts of the garden, and once the nest has been vacated it can be checked for any unhatched eggs which may have been missed, or young which have died when almost fully grown.

There are a few variations and exceptions to the above. Tits, when laying, often cover the eggs with a pad of the nest lining so that the first egg or two can easily be overlooked, and as the full clutch may well be as many as 13 eggs, patience when establishing clutch size is essential. Owls lay their eggs at intervals of forty-eight hours or more, and incubation normally starts with the laying of the first egg, so that later in the season the nest may contain young of various ages and eggs which are still capable of hatching. The success rate of owls varies tremendously according to the amount of food available, and the smaller young have a habit of 'disappearing' if times are hard. One may suspect cannibalism, but it is perhaps more charitable (and certainly more accurate) merely to record the reduced brood size and leave the question of the fate of the missing birds unanswered.

Many garden bird species are double brooded, a few, like the Swallow and Blackbird, may produce three or even more, and most will produce a new nest if the first attempt fails. Look for second broods 7–14 days after the fledging of the preceding brood or 4–6 days following a failure, and if you are certain that the same adult birds are involved, pin the two cards together. Records of failed nests are just as important as those for successes; if you send in details of only 'interesting' nests or only successful efforts, it will severely bias the results of any future analysis.

The completed cards should be returned to the BTO at the end of the breeding season. Each card will then become another link in the chain, and when sufficient records have accumulated, information on laying dates, clutch sizes and breeding success can be analysed to show variations between different geographical regions, habitats or years. With a healthy sample of cards each year, it is now possible to look at a group of 'indicator' species selected to cover a variety of important breeding habitats and utilising a variety of food resources. In this way we may detect any marked changes in breeding performance caused by environmental factors such as harmful chemicals.

Seasonal occurrences of some common garden birds together with details of the duration of breeding seasons and number of broods for those species which nest regularly. The width of the bars indicates the relative numbers of birds in the garden throughout the year.

	number of broods	Jan	Feb	Mar	Apr	May	Jun	Jul	Aug	Sep	Oct	Nov	Dec
Collared Dove	2–4												
Tawny Owl	1												
Swift	1												
Great Spotted Woodpecker	1												
Swallow	2(–3)												
House Martin	2–3												
Wren	2												
Dunnock	2–3												
Robin	2												
Blackbird	2–4												
Song Thrush	2–3												
Redwing													
Mistle Thrush	1–2												
Blackcap	2												
Spotted Flycatcher	2												
Blue Tit	1(–2)												
Great Tit	1(–2)												
Nuthatch	1												
Starling	1–2												
House Sparrow	2–3												
Chaffinch	1(–2)												
Brambling													
Greenfinch	2												
Siskin													

brackets in col. 2 refer to occasional subsequent broods

⬤ regular nestbox user
◖ occasional nestbox user
• a few clutches begun
○ small to moderate numbers
● periods of greater egg-laying activity

193

Telling one from another

During the summer months most of our observations will necessarily be of the breeding birds or of their young, but interesting changes in behaviour, some of them perhaps adaptations brought about as a result of human activities, may take place at any time.

One difficulty which is likely to present itself during any study is the identity of individual birds. In a small garden a regular Robin or Blackbird may be distinguished by its extreme tameness, by some peculiarity in its behaviour or maybe by some small abnormality in its plumage, in much the same way that each individual sheep in his flock is known to a good shepherd. However, at the end of the summer, when the season's crop of young birds is in evidence, or in midwinter when the starving birds from the surrounding area converge on the food which is being provided, the situation is very different.

To overcome this difficulty a system of marking the birds with rings originated over seventy years ago, and this technique has resulted in the accumulation of a vast amount of information which could not possibly have been gathered in any other way.

An eye to the main chance

During the last twenty years the tits have learned not only how to open milk bottles, but how to differentiate between the various grades of milk by selecting the correct coloured bottle cap. Siskins have solved the problem of what to do when the supply of alder seed is exhausted by coming into gardens for peanuts and fat, and more recently Grey Herons (above) have discovered that even tiny ponds in suburban gardens may provide a meal of goldfish, frogs or newts.

Many garden birds sunbathe but the Blackbird is the one most often seen in the typical posture, with wings and tail spread, gape open and feathers ruffled, especially near the preen gland. The precise function is not fully understood, but sunbathing does aid changes in the organic liquid on the feathers and helps with temperature regulation. Sunbathing birds get very incautious and may be approached closely.

Ringing as a source of information

The rings are made in a variety of sizes so that everything from a Goldcrest to a Mute Swan can be fitted with a ring of the appropriate size, and the operators have to undergo a thorough training under the eyes of at least two qualified ringers before being granted a government licence through the BTO to work alone.

The birds are either trapped or netted as adults, again using methods which have been adequately tested to ensure that the birds come to no harm, or the rings may be fitted to the nestlings before they have left the nest. This latter method is particularly valuable, since it records the actual birthplace of the ringed bird. Each ring has its own serial number and the ringer is required to enter opposite each number on a form the species, its age and sex where possible, the date of ringing and the location; from time to time certain other information may be called for which will require the ringer to weigh and measure the birds, or perhaps to record the progress of the moult, but the basic requirements are those given above. Each form or schedule holds fifty ring numbers and when these rings have all been fitted the completed schedule is returned to the BTO where it is filed.

195

```
                                                           GBT   17303R
        STURNUS VULGARIS
Species:  STARLING                         SPV                   15820

Age/Sex: 1 YEAR +                          4

Ringing Information:
        1  FEB  63  ±               53 59'N    1  5'W    ±

        YORK,

- - - -NORTH YORKSHIRE, ENGLAND - - - - - - - - - - - - - - - - - GBNY- -
Finding Information:
        1   JUN  81  (REPORT)       54 43'N   20 38'E    ±

        GUR'EVSK,

        KALININGRAD, U.S.S.R.                                    SU01
Finder:                               Finding Details:
        MOSCOW                        261-
                                      FRESHLY DEAD
                                      TAKEN BY CAT
                                      SAID FOUND ON 1.6.81,
                                      BUT SUSPECT.
                                      Distance:    Direction:    Duration:
                                      1409 KM      87 DEG        6695 DAYS
Ringer:
        BOOTHAM SCHOOL                             Batch:
BTO 1. File Copy.                                  150881    RH    RAC
```

Left: everyone who finds a ringed bird and sends the details to the Ringing Office at the BTO will receive a recovery computer printout. The form illustrated shows the fortunes of an adult Starling ringed at York during the severe winter weather of early 1963, and killed by a cat eighteen years later near Kaliningrad, Russia.

When a ringed bird is recovered – it may be a Chaffinch deposited on the doorstep by the owner's cat, a Wigeon from Russia or a Swallow from South Africa, or it may even be a bird bearing a ring of foreign origin since many countries now operate their own ringing schemes – the ring or its details should be returned to the BTO. If the bird is alive and is to be released, the number only should be recorded and passed on to the Trust, giving details of the location and date of the event. If the bird is dead, also give if possible the circumstances which caused the bird's death, e.g. killed by cat, collided with overhead wires, etc., when returning the ring. The British ringing scheme is in constant touch with the organisers of all the foreign schemes including those of Eastern Europe, and in due course both the ringer and the finder of the ringed bird will be informed of all the relevant details. Few garden bird enthusiasts are likely to be ringers, but by reporting any ringed birds they too can help in the gathering of vital data, and every opportunity of recording the presence of a ringed bird should be taken. If a ringed bird becomes a regular visitor to the garden it may be possible to find a local ringer who is willing to catch and record the bird; he would almost certainly welcome the opportunity to ring the brood of Swallows in the garage or the Spotted Flycatchers in the ivy on the wall, as they are just as likely to produce a recovery in some remote African village as any other Swallow or flycatcher (see p. 197).

Right: At one time some amazing theories were put forward to explain the disappearance of Swallows in winter, such as hibernating in the mud of ponds. The truth is no less spectacular, as shown by this map of the recoveries of Swallows ringed in Britain 10,500 km away from their winter quarters in South Africa. Inset: Tools of the trade, showing how a small ring is applied using special pliers which have a range of holes suitable for different-sized rings.

The importance of ringing

Distant foreign recoveries are, of course, the most glamorous part of the ringing scheme, but in the study of birds ringing has many other

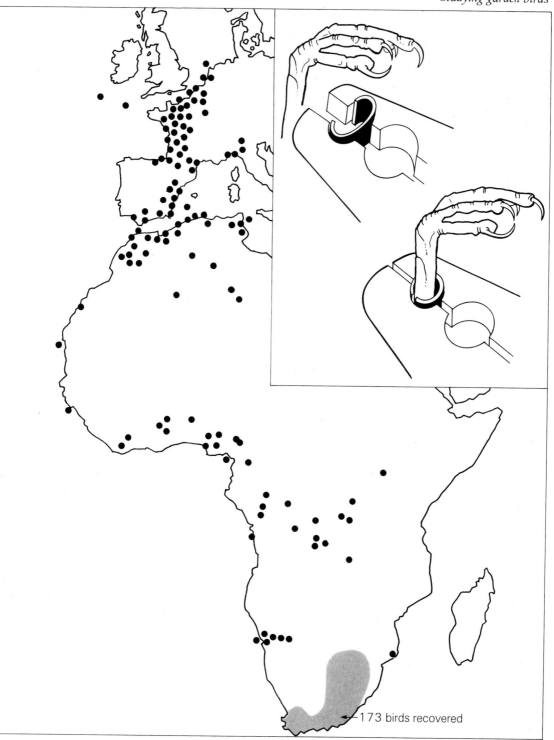

173 birds recovered

197

uses. Without this important research tool we should know little of the age which a bird may hope to attain. There are considerable differences even between some of the smaller species; Swifts, for example, have a longer life expectancy than most birds of similar size, in spite of the fact that they spend most of their lives on the wing and might be expected to use more energy than the more sedentary species. Fluctuations in population levels due to hard winters or difficult conditions during migration, problems when numbers reach unacceptably high levels (such as Bullfinches in fruit growing areas, Cormorants or Oystercatchers in fishing communities, gulls on inland waters), are all examples of cases where ringing can help to establish the numbers and the pattern of local movement, but it is in the field of conservation that it has proved most valuable in recent years.

Conservation through the garden

When plans are drawn up to 'develop' an area rich in bird life or unique as a breeding area for certain species, local ornithologists are usually well aware of the implications. They will often know already how many Dartford Warblers breed on a certain strip of heathland or the number of waders using a particular estuary, but opinions and rough estimates are of little use when an official inquiry and possibly even a decision by the Secretary of State for the Environment become necessary. We then need facts, facts supported by census work in the area over a number of years, by duck counts and wader counts carried out assiduously throughout the winter months. The various census techniques complement each other and the resulting analysis is likely to carry far more weight than any unsupported statement. It is surprising just how much of this 'basic' information originates from studies conducted in gardens, a habitat that is increasing annually in its importance as a food source and breeding place for our bird life.

Common and Scientific Names of Birds

This list gives the vernacular and scientific names of all species mentioned in the text and/or recorded by the BTO's Garden Bird Feeding Survey as taking food or water over the ten winters from 1970/71 to 1979/80; the latter is indicated by an asterisk (*). The order of names is that compiled by Professor K.H. Voous of Amsterdam, which is used in the majority of modern Field Guides and can be found in BTO Guide No.13 *A Species List of British and Irish Birds* (edited by Robert Hudson, Tring, 1978).

Cormorant   *Phalacrocorax carbo*
Grey Heron   *Ardea cinerea**
Mute Swan   *Cygnus olor**
Bewick's Swan   *Cygnus columbianus*
Canada Goose   *Branta canadensis**
Ruddy Shelduck   *Tadorna ferruginea**
Wigeon   *Anas penelope*
Teal   *Anas crecca**
Mallard   *Anas platyrhynchos**
Pochard   *Aythya ferina**
Black Kite   *Milvus migrans*
Red Kite   *Milvus milvus*
Hen Harrier   *Circus cyaneus*
Goshawk   *Accipiter gentilis*
Sparrowhawk   *Accipiter nisus**
Buzzard   *Buteo buteo**
Kestrel   *Falco tinnunculus**
Merlin   *Falco columbarius**
Peregrine   *Falco peregrinus*
Red-legged Partridge   *Alectoris rufa**
Grey Partridge   *Perdix perdix**
Quail   *Coturnix coturnix*
Pheasant   *Phasianus colchicus**
Golden Pheasant   *Chrysolophus pictus*
Lady Amherst's Pheasant   *Chrysolophus amherstiae**
Reeves' Pheasant   *Syrmaticus reevesii**
Water Rail   *Rallus aquaticus**
Moorhen   *Gallinula chloropus**
Coot   *Fulica atra**
Oystercatcher   *Haematopus ostralegus*
Lapwing   *Vanellus vanellus**
Snipe   *Gallinago gallinago**
Woodcock   *Scolopax rusticola**
Redshank   *Tringa totanus**
Black-headed Gull   *Larus ridibundus**
Common Gull   *Larus canus**
Lesser Black-backed Gull   *Larus fuscus**
Herring Gull   *Larus argentatus**

Great Black-backed Gull   *Larus marinus**
Feral Pigeon   *Columba livia**
Stock Dove   *Columba oenas**
Woodpigeon   *Columba palumbus**
Collared Dove   *Streptopelia decaocto**
Turtle Dove   *Streptopelia turtur**
Barbary Dove   *Streptopelia 'risoria'**
Budgerigar   *Melopsittacus undulatus**
Ring-necked Parakeet   *Psittacula krameri**
Cuckoo   *Cuculus canorus*
Barn Owl   *Tyto alba**
Little Owl   *Athene noctua**
Tawny Owl   *Strix aluco**
Nightjar   *Caprimulgus europaeus*
Swift   *Apus apus*
Kingfisher   *Alcedo atthis**
Hoopoe   *Upupa epops*
Wryneck   *Jynx torquilla*
Green Woodpecker   *Picus viridis**
Great Spotted Woodpecker   *Dendrocopos major**
Lesser Spotted Woodpecker   *Dendrocopos minor**
Woodlark   *Lullula arborea**
Skylark   *Alauda arvensis**
Sand Martin   *Riparia riparia*
Swallow   *Hirundo rustica*
House Martin   *Delichon urbica*
Tree Pipit   *Anthus trivialis**
Meadow Pipit   *Anthus pratensis**
Rock Pipit   *Anthus spinoletta**
Yellow Wagtail   *Motacilla flava**
Grey Wagtail   *Motacilla cinerea**
Pied Wagtail   *Motacilla alba**
Waxwing   *Bombycilla garrulus**
Dipper   *Cinclus cinclus**
Wren   *Troglodytes troglodytes**
Dunnock   *Prunella modularis**
Robin   *Erithacus rubecula**
Nightingale   *Luscinia megarhynchos*
Bluethroat   *Luscinia svecica*
Black Redstart   *Phoenicurus ochruros**
Redstart   *Phoenicurus phoenicurus**
Stonechat   *Saxicola torquata**
Wheatear   *Oenanthe oenanthe**
Ring Ouzel   *Turdus torquatus**
Blackbird   *Turdus merula**
Fieldfare   *Turdus pilaris**
Song Thrush   *Turdus philomelos**
Redwing   *Turdus iliacus**
Mistle Thrush   *Turdus viscivorus**

Dartford Warbler *Sylvia undata*
Lesser Whitethroat *Sylvia curruca*
Whitethroat *Sylvia communis**
Garden Warbler *Sylvia borin**
Blackcap *Sylvia atricapilla**
Wood Warbler *Phylloscopus sibilatrix**
Chiffchaff *Phylloscopus collybita**
Willow Warbler *Phylloscopus trochilus**
Goldcrest *Regulus regulus**
Firecrest *Regulus ignicapillus**
Spotted Flycatcher *Muscicapa striata**
Red-breasted Flycatcher *Ficedula parva*
Pied Flycatcher *Ficedula hypoleuca**
Long-tailed Tit *Aegithalos caudatus**
Marsh Tit *Parus palustris**
Willow Tit *Parus montanus**
Crested Tit *Parus cristatus**
Coal Tit *Parus ater**
Blue Tit *Parus caeruleus**
Great Tit *Parus major**
Nuthatch *Sitta europaea**
Treecreeper *Certhia familiaris**
Great Grey Shrike *Lanius excubitor**
Blue Jay *Cyanocitta cristata*
Jay *Garrulus glandarius**
Magpie *Pica pica**
Jackdaw *Corvus monedula**
Rook *Corvus frugilegus**
Carrion (or Hooded) Crow *Corvus corone**
Raven *Corvus corax**

Starling *Sturnus vulgaris**
Zebra Finch *Poephila guttata**
Cut-throat *Amadina fasciata**
House Sparrow *Passer domesticus**
Tree Sparrow *Passer montanus**
Orange Bishop *Euplectes orix**
Chaffinch *Fringilla coelebs**
Brambling *Fringilla montifringilla**
Canary *Serinus canarius**
Greenfinch *Carduelis chloris**
Goldfinch *Carduelis carduelis**
Siskin *Carduelis spinus**
Linnet *Carduelis cannabina**
Twite *Carduelis flavirostris**
Redpoll *Carduelis flammea**
Common Crossbill *Loxia curvirostra**
Bullfinch *Pyrrhula pyrrhula**
Hawfinch *Coccothraustes coccothraustes**
Yellow-rumped (or Myrtle) Warbler *Dendroica coronata*
Harris Sparrow *Zonotrichia querula*
White-crowned Sparrow *Zonotrichia leucophrys*
Lapland Bunting *Calcarius lapponicus**
Snow Bunting *Plectrophenax nivalis**
Yellowhammer *Emberiza citrinella**
Cirl Bunting *Emberiza cirlus**
Reed Bunting *Emberiza schoeniclus**
Corn Bunting *Miliaria calandra**
Cardinal *Cardinalis cardinalis**

Further Reading

The selected list of books and journals below may be consulted for identification purposes or for further information on garden birds.

ARMSTRONG, E.A. 1955. *The Wren*. Collins, London.

BUCKS, F.D. (Ed.). 1964. Natural History of the Garden of Buckingham Palace. *Proc. S. Lond. Ent. Nat. Hist. Soc. 1963*.

CAMPBELL, B. and I.J. FERGUSON-LEES. 1972. *A Field Guide to Birds' Nests*. Constable, London.

CHINERY, M. 1977. *The Natural History of the Garden*. Collins, London.

COARD, P.T. 1975, 1976, 1978. 'Birds Drinking and Bathing', in *Devon Birds* 28: 72–74; 29: 42–50; 31: 37–43.

COOPER, J.E. and J.T. ELEY. 1979. *First Aid and Care of Wild Birds*. David and Charles, Newton Abbot.

CORBET, G.B. and H.N. SOUTHERN. 1977. *The Handbook of British Mammals*. Blackwell, Oxford.

DOBINSON, H.M. 1976. *Bird Count*. Penguin, Harmondsworth.

EASTMAN, R. 1969. *The Kingfisher*. Collins, London.

FISHER, J. and J.J.M. FLEGG. 1974. *Watching Birds*. Poyser, Berkhamsted.

FLEGG, J.J.M. and D.E. GLUE. 1971. *Nestboxes*. BTO Field Guide No.3, Tring.

GOODWIN, D. 1967. *Pigeons and Doves of the World*. Trustees of the British Museum (Natural History), London.

HARRISON, C.J.O. 1975. *A Field Guide to the Nests, Eggs and Nestlings of British and European Birds*. Collins, London.

HEINZEL, H., R.S.R. FITTER and J.L.F. PARSLOW. 1972. *The Birds of Britain and Europe*. Collins, London.

HOLLOM, P.A.D. 1952. *The Popular Handbook of British Birds*. Witherby, London.

LACK, D. 1943. *The Life of the Robin*. Witherby, London.

LACK, D. 1973. *Swifts in a Tower*. Chapman and Hall, London.

LEACH, I.H. 1981. 'Wintering Blackcaps in Britain and Ireland', in *Bird Study* 28: 5–14.

MAYER-GROSS, H. 1970. *Nest Record Scheme*. BTO Field Guide No.12, Tring.

MEAD, C.J. 1974. *Bird Ringing*. BTO Guide No.16, Tring.

MITCHELL, A. 1974. *A Field Guide to the Trees of Britain and Northern Europe*. Collins, London.

MURTON, R.K. and E.N. WRIGHT. 1968. *The Problems of Birds as Pests*. Academic Press, London.

MURTON, R.K. 1971. *Man and Birds*. Collins, London.

NEWTON, I. 1972. *Finches*. Collins, London.

NEWTON, I. 1979. *Population Ecology of Raptors*. Poyser, Berkhamsted.

PEMBERTON, J.E. 1981. *Birdwatcher's Yearbook 1982*. Buckingham Press, Buckingham.

PERRINS, C.M. 1979. *British Tits*. Collins, London.

RICHARDS, A.J. 1980. *The Birdwatcher's A–Z*. David and Charles, Newton Abbot.

RIDDIFORD, N. and P. FINDLEY. 1981. *Seasonal Movements of Summer Migrants*. BTO Guide No.18, Tring.

SHARROCK, J.T.R. 1976. *The Atlas of Breeding Birds in Britain and Ireland*. Poyser, Berkhamsted.

SIMMS, E. 1975. *Birds of Town and Suburb*. Collins, London.

SIMMS, E. 1978. *British Thrushes*. Collins, London.

SNOW, D.W. 1958. *A Study of Blackbirds*. George Allen and Unwin, London.

SOPER, T. 1965. *The New Bird Table Book*. David and Charles, Newton Abbot.

SUMMERS-SMITH, J.D. 1963. *The House Sparrow*. Collins, London.

THOMSON, A. LANDSBOROUGH 1964. *A New Dictionary of Birds*. Nelson, London.

THORNTON, J. 1981. *DIY Bird Table*. RSPB, Sandy.

WEAVER, P. 1981. *The Bird-Watchers' Dictionary*. Poyser, Calton.

WELTY, J.C. 1975. *The Life of Birds*. W.B. Saunders, Philadelphia.

WITHERBY, H.F., F.C.R. JOURDAIN, N.F. TICEHURST and B.W. TUCKER. 1938–41. *The Handbook of British Birds Vols I–V*. Witherby, London.

Plants useful to Birds

Trees and shrubs for birds in gardens

Genus and species/variety	Type of tree	Colour of fruit	Approx. ht (cm)	Notes
Aronia arbutifolia	D	crimson	120	Suckering shrub with good autumn foliage
A. prunifolia	D	purple	120	
A. melanocarpa	D	black	90	
Aucuba japonica (several varieties)	E	black	300	Good in shade
Berberis acuminata (*veitchii*)	E	black	200	Shrub or hedge
B. aggregata	D	coral	120	Prolific
B. coryi	D	red	100	For small garden
B. darwinii	E	blue/black	180	Indispensable
B. gagnepainii	E	black	125	For small garden or as hedge
B. linearifolia	E	orange	200	
B. polyantha	D	red	150	Good autumn foliage
B. prattii	D	red	120	Heavy cropper
B. stenophylla	E	red	200	Makes fine thorny hedge
B. thunbergii	D	red	150	
B. thunbergii atropurpurea	D	red	200	Purple foliage
B. verruculosa	E	black	125	Good hedge
B. wilsonae	D	red	150	For smaller garden
B. yunnanensis	D	red	150	Attractive in autumn
Callicarpa bodinieri giraldii (*giraldiana*)	D	lilac	150	Plant 2 or 3 to ensure pollination
Coriaria terminalis xanthocarpa	D	amber	90	Dies down each winter
Cornus mas	D	red	100	Slow to produce fruit
C. sanguinea	D	black	200	
Cotoneaster adpressus	D	red	prostrate	Good on banks
C. bullatus	D	crimson	300	Shrub or small tree
C. buxifolius	E	red	prostrate	For small garden
C. conspicuus decorus	E	red	50	Free fruiting, for banks
C. dammeri	E	coral	prostrate	Ground cover
C. divaricatus	D	red	120	Very reliable
C. franchetii sternianus	E	orange	200	Highly recommended
C. frigidus	D	red	300	Fast growing
C. henryanus	E	crimson	300	Similar to *C. salicifolius* (q.v.)
C. horizontalis	E	red	200	Indispensable for walls
C. lacteus	E	red	180	Late; fruit lasts well
C. pannosus	E	red	120	Later and smaller than *C. franchetii*
C. salicifolius flocossus	semi-E	red	300	Graceful and prolific
C. simonsii	E	red	300	Screening hedge
C. thymifolius (*microphyllus*)	E	red	prostrate	Draping walls and banks
C. watereri	semi-E	red	300	A hybrid; several forms
Crataegus monogyna	D	red	500	As a hedge or a tree; double hawthorns do not bear fruit
Daphne mezereum	D	red	80	Daphnes require heavy soil, good on chalk
D. mezereum alba	D	yellow	80	
Frangula alnus	D	black	400	Better on acid soils
Gaultheria procumbens	E	red	10	Ground cover; acid soils
G. shallon	E	red/brown	50	Rampant cover; sun or shade
Hippophae rhamnoides	D	orange	200	Excellent seaside shrub
Ilex altaclarensis 'Golden King'	E	red	indefinite	If alternative varieties of holly are offered insist on a female plant
I. aquifolium 'Pyramidalis'	E	red	indefinite	
Laurus nobilis	E	black	300	Female plant required
Ligustrum vulgare	E	black	250	Avoid *L. ovalifolium*
Lonicera henryi	E	black	–	Rampant climber, provides good nesting sites
L. periclymenum	D	red	–	Native honeysuckle

Genus and species/variety	Type of tree	Colour of fruit	Approx. ht (cm)	Notes
L. pileata	semi-E	violet	150	Shrub; good in shade
Malus 'Golden Hornet'	D	yellow	500 +	All Malus make ideal small trees; the fruit often persists into midwinter
M. 'John Downie'	D	red and yellow	500	
M. 'Red Sentinel'	D	red	500	
M. 'Wisley'	D	crimson	500	
Mahonia japonica (bealei)	E	black	200	Two slightly different plants, both excellent
Photinia villosa	D	red	300	Small tree for acid soils
Prunus laurocerasus 'Otto Luyken'	E	black	125	Attractive small laurel
P. spinosa (sloe)	D	black	500	Best as impenetrable hedge
Pyracantha angustifolia	E	orange	400	North walls, hedge or shrub. All pyracantha are free fruiting
P. atalantioides	E	scarlet	500	
P. 'Orange Glow'	E	orange	500	
P. rogersiana 'Flava'	E	yellow	400	
Rhamnus cathartica	D	black	400	Does well on chalk
Rubus laciniatus	D	black	–	There is a thornless variety
R. phoenicolasius	D	amber	200	Unusual and attractive
Sambucus nigra	D	black	600 +	All birds love it
S. racemosa	D	red	400	Flourishes in bleak areas
Sarcococca hookerana digyna	E	black	40	Ground cover
Sorbus aria	D	orange/red	500 +	Good on chalk
S. aucuparia	D	red	800	Many varieties, all good
S. 'Embley'	D	red	800	Origin uncertain but a most spectacular tree
S. 'Joseph Rock'	D	amber	800	Another outstanding tree of uncertain origin
S. sargentiana	D	red	800	An improvement on the common mountain ash
Stranvaesia davidiana	E	red or yellow	400	Good in cities
Symphoricarpos chenaultii 'Hancock'	D	purple	80	Good low cover
Vaccinium corymbosum	D	black	150	Acid soils only
V. vitis-idaea	E	red	15	Acid soil; ground cover
Viburnum lantana	D	black	200	Good on chalk
V. opulus	D	red	200	Wet or boggy situations
Vitis vinifera 'Brandt'	D	purple	–	Hardy hybrid grapevine

Note: All berberis and cotoneasters will flourish on any garden soil, and being unaffected by salt-laden winds are excellent seaside shrubs.

In the column headed 'Type of tree', 'E' stands for evergreen and 'D' for deciduous.

There are over eighty varieties of cypress ranging from tiny dwarfs of under 50 cm when full grown to giant trees. With the exception of the true dwarfs all are useful as roosting and nesting places and as windbreaks in cold areas. Any nursery will be able to offer a wide variety.

In addition there are a few trees and shrubs mentioned in the text which are useful for reasons other than for the fruit which they provide. These are given below.

Genus and species/variety	Type of tree	Approx. ht (cm)	Notes
Escallonia (numerous hybrids and varieties)	E	150	Excellent seaside shrubs
Garrya elliptica	E	400	North wall shrub for early nesting thrushes
Juniperus communis (numerous varieties)	E		All tough, good on chalk or by the sea
Pinus pinaster	E		Front-line seaside windbreak
P. radiata	E		Useful on the coast; somewhat tender inland
Quercus ilex (evergreen oak)	E		Can be clipped as a hedge around coastal gardens
Salix caprea	D	400	Early spring flowers attract insects
Tamarix gallica	D		Seaside cover particularly attractive to small migrants

Note: No height is given for the seaside trees since the amount of wind which they have to tolerate is usually the controlling factor.

Useful Addresses

Organisations concerned with birds and nature conservation

British Trust for Ornithology (BTO)
Beech Grove, Tring, Hertfordshire HP23 5NR.
The Trust collects the facts on which the welfare of our birds depends, through fieldwork undertaken by a network of thousands of birdwatchers under the direction of a small professional staff. It organises the Ringing Scheme, maps bird distribution, and investigates their breeding and feeding biology through on-going surveys such as the Common Birds Census, Nest Record Scheme, Waterways Bird Survey, Birds of Estuaries Enquiry, Garden Bird Feeding Survey and numerous special enquiries. Finance comes from membership subscriptions, government and other grants. Membership details are available from the Administrator at the above address.

British Ornithologists' Union (BOU)
c/o The Zoological Society of London, Regent's Park, London NW1 4RY.
The senior ornithological society in Great Britain. Its chief aim is the advancement of the science of ornithology on a worldwide scale.

Irish Wildbird Conservancy (IWC)
South View, Church Road, Greystones, Co. Wicklow, Ireland.
Ireland's largest voluntary body concerned with the protection and conservation of wildlife in the Republic.

Mammal Society
Harvest House, 62 London Road, Reading RG1 5AS.
Amalgamates the fieldwork and research activities of both amateur and professional mammalogists.

Nature Conservancy Council (NCC)
Great Britain Headquarters: 20 Belgrave Square, London SW1X 8PY.
A government body fostering awareness in Great Britain of the importance of nature conservation, which it achieves through research, reserves and grants.

Royal Society for Nature Conservation (RSNC)
The Green, Nettleham, Lincoln LN2 2NR.
Co-ordinates and advises the country-wide network of County Trusts on the acquisition and management of reserves.

Royal Society for the Protection of Birds (RSPB)
The Lodge, Sandy, Bedfordshire SG19 2DL.
A voluntary organisation which aims to protect wild birds and their habitats through enforcement of the law, research and managing a number of bird reserves.

Scottish Ornithologists' Club (SOC)
21 Regent Terrace, Edinburgh EH7 5BT.
Co-ordinates ornithological studies in Scotland through a network of local branches.

Wildfowl Trust (WT)
Slimbridge, Gloucester GL2 7BT.
A voluntary organisation which maintains unique collections of wildfowl, containing many rare and endangered species, at reserves which also act as wildfowl winter refuges. In addition it undertakes research including national wildfowl counts.

World Wildlife Fund (WWF)
29 Greville Street, London EC1N 8AX.
Aims to create awareness of threats to the natural environment and to generate moral and financial support for conservation on a worldwide scale.

Manufacturers and suppliers of garden bird products

J.E. Haith, Park Street, Cleethorpes, S. Humberside DN35 7NF.

Nerine Nurseries, Welland, near Malvern, Hereford and Worcester WR13 6LN.

Pippaware, 70 Wakeman Road, London NW10 5DH.

Rikden, R. Dendy, 2 Aultone Yard, Aultone Way, Carshalton, Surrey SM5 2LH.

Royal Society for the Protection of Birds (see above).

Scottish National Institute for the War Blinded, Linburn, Wilkieston by Kirknewton, West Lothian EH27 8DU.

Jamie Wood Products Ltd, Cross Street, Polegate, East Sussex BN26 6BN.

Manufacturers' products and prices are constantly changing, but up-to-date details can usually be traced through *Bird Study* and *BTO News*, both published by the BTO (see above).

Journals

British Birds is an independent monthly journal for birdwatchers. Membership details are available from Fountains, Blunham, Bedford MK44 3NJ.

Birds is published quarterly by the RSPB (see above), who also produce a sales catalogue.

Index

Page numbers in *italic* refer to the illustrations.

Picture Credits

The British Trust for Ornithology and Macmillan London Ltd gratefully acknowledge the kindness of the following individuals and collections in making available black-and-white photographs reproduced in this book: Anthony J. Bond 46. Kevin Carlson 56, 180. R.J. Chandler 73. C. Crosthwaite 195. Bruce Coleman Ltd/photo R. Tidman 70. Eric Hosking 12, 59, 60, 141, 143, 162, 189. E.A. Janes 95, 116, 132, 148, 178. Richard T. Mills 27, 34, 49, 55, 57, 66, 93, 113, 157, 167. A.N.H. Peach 10. J. Russell 99. Colin Smale 62. Robert T. Smith 65, 76, 121, 171. B.S. Turner viii, 3, 15, 37, 68, 124. M.C. Wilkes 95, 103, 130, 136, 146, 153, 181. Stuart Wilton 177. J.F. Young 30.

Colour plates: D. Bodenham 88 above left and right. Bruce Coleman Ltd/photo Roger Wilmshurst 81; photo Dennis Green 83; photo Hans Reinhard 87. Eric and David Hosking 82 below, 84, 86. Royal Society for the Protection of Birds/photo Michael W. Richards 82 above. Harry Smith Horticultural Photographic Collection 88 below left and right.

Illustrators: Berry/Fallon Design 6, 92, 93, 94, 104, 105, 106, 107, 152, 157, 193, 197. Chris and Hilary Evans 7, 54, 64, 67, 69, 74, 118, 120, 121, 123, 131 left, 135, 151, 153, 155 above, 159, 164, 168, 184, 185, 186. Pete Ferris 4. Alan Harris 9, 18, 19, 20, 42, 48, 53, 78, 90, 91, 101, 109, 110, 115, 119, 126, 127, 128, 131 right, 134, 140, 142, 144, 145, 147, 150, 155 below, 160, 172, 174, 175, 182, 188, 194, 198. Richard Holling 16, 44, 51. Nina Roberts 23, 25, 28, 29, 32, 35, 36, 39, 40, 41, 72.